Essential
Jamaica

by

ANNIE WILSON

Annie Wilson is an experienced
travel writer and researcher
who has produced guides to holiday
destinations throughout the world.

Produced by AA Publishing

Written by Annie Wilson
Peace and Quiet section
by Paul Sterry
Series Adviser: Ingrid Morgan
Series Controller: Nia Williams
Copy Editor: Dilys Jones

Edited, designed and produced by
AA Publishing. Maps © The
Automobile Association 1992.

Distributed in the United Kingdom
by the Publishing Division of The
Automobile Association, Fanum
House, Basingstoke, Hampshire,
RG21 2EA.

The contents of this publication are
believed correct at the time of
printing. Nevertheless, the
publishers cannot accept
responsibility for errors or
omissions, nor for changes in details
given. We have tried to ensure
accuracy in this guide, but things
do change and we would be
grateful if readers would advise us
of any inaccuracies they may
encounter.

A CIP catalogue record for this
book is available from the British
Library.

ISBN 0 7495 0309 2

Published by The Automobile
Association.

Typesetting: Avonset, Midsomer
Norton, Bath
Colour separation: LC Repro & Son
Ltd, Aldermaston.
Printed in Italy by Printers SRL,
Trento

Front cover picture: Ocho Rios

This book employs a simple rating system to help choose which places to visit:

◆◆◆   do not miss

◆◆   see if you can

◆   worth seeing if you have time

INTRODUCTION

A Caribbean island in the sun – the idyllic
images this conjures up are really there to be
found in Jamaica. And much more, if you take
the time to explore. Of course, there are the
seductive, soft white beaches, lapped by
limpid aquamarine seas and fringed by
palms, where you can bask in the sun. And
the swish hotels where the guests want for
nothing. But these are just part of the
kaleidoscope of alternatives that Jamaica can
offer visitors. Jamaica's vibrant character
reflects its rich history, colourful culture and
natural beauty, which can make your holiday
a truly unique experience.

What strikes the eye first is the sumptuous
scenery. Jamaica is dominated by rugged
highlands, rising to the high, hazy peaks of
the Blue Mountains in the east. In places the
slopes plunge almost directly down to the
coast; steep valleys are cut by the clear
waters of many rivers, which spill over rocks
in wonderful waterfalls. The hillsides are

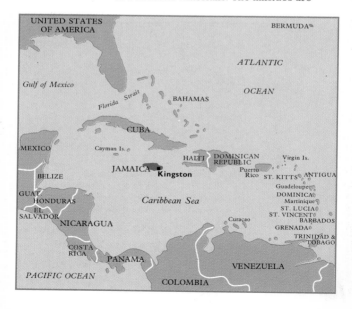

smothered in tropical forests, especially in the north, which is much greener than the south. Most visitors head for the north coast, and its sparkling strips of silvery sand hugged by hotels. This is where the busy, lively resorts are, and the cruise ports of Montego Bay and Ocho Rios. There is also the tranquil, and much less touristy, Port Antonio, set amid some of the island's loveliest scenery and beaches. On the west coast is Jamaica's most stunning beach, and its most relaxed resort – Negril.

The south of the island has a very different atmosphere – it is scarcely touched by tourism as yet. Towards the east is the sprawling, noisy, dusty capital, Kingston, with its impressive harbour set against a beautiful backdrop of mountains. In the cool highlands inland is the genteel town of Mandeville. And the coast boasts quiet, secluded spots like the aptly-named Treasure Beach, and the quaint little town of Black River, backed by swampland which has a wealth of wildlife.

It is a shame to stick to the popular spots along the north and west coast, or worse, to stay put in your hotel for two weeks. You may have a fabulous time, but this can give a rather slick, superficial view of Jamaica, and you miss out on its real and diverse character. It is possible to meet Jamaicans who can make your day, or even your whole holiday, a joy. They are justifiably proud of their beautiful island and they want their guests to enjoy the best of Jamaica. So where is the hostility, the violence, and the crime that became associated with Jamaica some years ago? Visitors can rest easy about any rumours of Jamaica's dark heart – these were mostly the result of political tensions, inflamed during election times. As a visitor, you are unlikely to encounter any difficulties of this sort, or feel threatened, if you take care, as you would anywhere, and are not foolish enough to venture into the ghetto areas of Kingston. Just show respect to the locals and their way of life – remember that 'respect' is a much-used (and valued) word in Jamaica – and you will find them friendlier than people in many other parts of the world.

Remember though, that Jamaica is a Third World country. Life isn't always easy for Jamaicans – although they seem so full of *joie de vivre* – and the island has known plenty of hardship in its turbulent and chequered past. Its heritage stems from a rich stew of different influences, including colonisation by the Spanish and then the British, both of whom imported slaves from Africa to work their plantations, and incursions by others (not least the buccaneers and pirates) who realised the attractions and strategic value of the island. As a result you will find people of every colour and ethnic origin – from African to Chinese, Indian, Jewish, Arabic and European. Their national independence motto is 'Out of many, one people'. The years of British rule have left an unmistakable legacy, from the educational and judiciary systems to cricket and driving on the left – there are also lots of familiar names, like Surrey, Middlesex and Cornwall, the three counties into which Jamaica is divided. But these names are mixed with others of Spanish and African origin. Even the language, though technically English, derives much from the melting pot of words, expressions and accents, so that the patois is practically incomprehensible to other English-speakers.

This island has enchanted visitors for centuries – from Christopher Columbus to Noël Coward, Errol Flynn to Paul McCartney. The spectacularly beautiful scenery is enriched by the vivid flowers and scent of vanilla, spice or jasmine wafting in the air. Your tastebuds will be sharpened by a tantalising array of local dishes, from piquant fresh fish to luscious fruits – and not forgetting the ubiquitous rum punches. And then, naturally, there are the hypnotic rhythms of the music, especially reggae. Jamaica seduces the body and soul – but if you want to take your intellect off the back-burner, it is well worth delving into the history, culture and legends of the island. Problems are forgotten here, and everything 'soon come' to those who relax into the laid-back rhythm of life. Then, without question, you will believe everything is 'irie', as they say in Jamaica.

BACKGROUND

Geography

Jamaica's landscapes are the stage on which its dramatic character unfolds.

It is the third largest island in the Caribbean, sitting 28 degrees north of the equator, 90 miles (145km) south of Cuba. Said to be shaped like a swimming turtle, Jamaica is about 145 miles (233km) long from Negril to Morant Point, and 50 miles (80km) at its widest point (north to south). A central backbone of mountains stretches from the west, along the curious pitted plateau of Cockpit Country, to the ethereal eastern peaks of the Blue Mountains. They reach heavenward through the clouds, rising to 7,402 feet (2,256m) only 10 miles (16km) from the coastal plain near Kingston. More than half the island lies 1,000 feet (300m) above the sparkling turquoise seas that surround it. In places it is honeycombed with impressive cave systems that show the oceanic origins of this landscape, which was thrust up from the sea-bed by volcanic activity millions of years ago. Although it is the sunshine that epitomises the warm character of the island, rainfall on the mountains and northern coast results in distinctive differences in the scenery. The highlands and slopes rising from the north coast are generally luxuriantly wooded; while the wider coastal plains along the south look much drier, with landscapes like the African savannah or Mediterranean scrub in many places.

Trees and bush vegetation proliferate all over Jamaica, even in the drier areas, but there are also many areas of grassy fields and plantations where the woods were cleared by Europeans in past centuries. Here cattle graze, or stand quietly in the cool shade of palm and mango trees, always accompanied by white egrets (a heron-like bird) which eat their ticks.

There are more than 120 rivers on the island, which tumble down through mountain gorges to the coastal plains and sea, swelled to raging torrents by high rains or reduced to boulder-strewn gullies in dry weather.

BACKGROUND

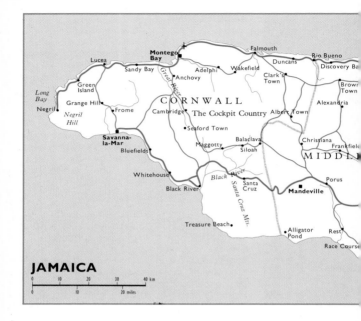

The island's beautiful beaches are a prime
tourist attraction. Many nestle in coves,
bordered by rocks and cliffs, and are
protected by coral reefs from which the pale
sands have been formed (as well as the
offshore cays and islets).

Towns and villages tend to be scruffy,
haphazard settlements. And the sophisticated
hotels along the north coast are in stark
contrast to the simple, shabby clapboard or
breeze-block homes with corrugated zinc
roofs in which most Jamiacans live. The tourist
development along the north coast is not
continuous; although it spreads out from the
resorts (especially Montego Bay, Ocho Rios
and the area between them), there are
stretches that are quite unspoilt. But you do
see touches of tourism that are missing from
the south coast – such as numerous craft stalls
beside the road, signs for rooms to rent or
restaurants, and simply more foreign white
faces. For a truly unspoilt taste of Jamaica,

BACKGROUND

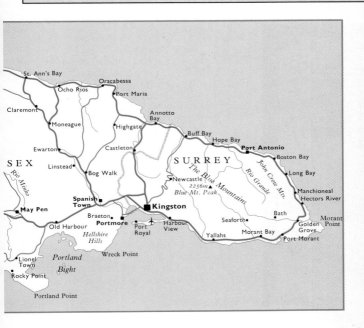

you must explore inland or the south.
However, from the north coast, you need only
go a few miles inland and into the hills to find
complete peace and superb panoramas –
typical rural Jamaica. The slopes are cloaked
in a confusion of jungly foliage; the tall trees
adorned with tangles of trailing creepers and
vines, and the dark green spangled with the
sizzling scarlet blooms of the flame of the
forest or poinciana trees. Along the roads are
scattered brightly-painted shacks, and groups
of locals sit gossiping and laughing outside
open bar-shops while goats wander around
nibbling the shrubs. Small patches of yams,
sweet peppers or citrus trees are cultivated
around the houses; donkeys, heavily-laden
with crops like sticks of sugar cane, vie with
battered buses packed to the roof-racks;
there is often a boy carrying a bucket of
water on his head or a man with a
precariously-balanced pile of bananas and
breadfruit; women sell exotic fruit like paw-

paw or ackee by the roadside, or wash clothes in the river and lay them out to dry on the hot rocks; a dreadlocked woolly-hatted Rasta may be glimpsed smoking *ganja*. And as you pass by, cute kids in school uniforms shout cheeky greetings. Most of life takes place outside in Jamaica.

Sugar cane, bananas, coffee and citrus fruit were introduced by the Spanish colonists and became important export crops. Sugar is still a major crop, and you will see big plantations with acres of long spear-like cane leaves waving in the breeze; sugar is also distilled into various types of famous Jamaica rum. The emerald-green banana palms can be seen growing everywhere in people's backyards, but the most extensive plantations are along the northeast coast. Coffee is grown in the mountains, and Blue Mountain coffee is world-renowned. Other cash crops include tobacco, coconuts, cocoa, pimento (a tree producing allspice – the only one of these that is a native of Jamaica), and *ganja* (marijuana, first introduced by workers from India) which, of course, is illegal.

Jamaica is one of the world's biggest bauxite producers, and this is vital to the island's economy, being one of its biggest export earners. However, the industry on which Jamaica relies most heavily is tourism. As such an important source of foreign exchange, in the light of the serious economic (and political) problems they have had to face, it is not surprising the government has worked hard to promote a positive image of late. Very many of the island's inhabitants are directly or indirectly employed by tourism, and even if locals see little of the spoils, they still want to ensure Jamaica remains attractive to visitors – whose money provides opportunities where there might be none in a country of high unemployment and poverty.

History
First Settlers
Jamaica's original inhabitants were Arawak Indians, who first arrived from South America in about AD650. Until the Spanish colonists

Left: wood carvings settled here centuries later, the Arawaks thrived on the island they called *Xaymaca* (meaning 'land of wood and water'). These Indians were a peaceful people who were skilled artisans, but all that remains of the Arawak culture are various artefacts and cave paintings found near village sites – and a few words like 'hammock' (which they invented, and wove from the cotton they grew), 'canoe', 'tobacco', 'barbecue' and 'hurricane'.

It was in 1494 that Christopher Columbus arrived at Jamaica, landing on the north coast and claiming the island in the name of the Spanish crown. He said it was the 'fairest island that eyes have beheld'. The Spanish colonists began arriving around 1510, and established their first settlement of Sevilla Nueva (New Seville) near St Ann's Bay in the north. But 25 years later they abandoned it for a more propitious site in the south: Villa de la Vega was the new capital, eventually to be simply called Spanish Town. Lying west of Kingston, it remained Jamaica's capital until 1872.

The island became a backwater of the Spanish colonies. There was no gold, as had been hoped, and it was used principally as a base to supply Spanish ships. But they did introduce some important crops, including sugar cane and bananas. The Spanish destroyed the native Arawak population: they were forced into hard labour, cruelly mistreated and also affected by European diseases to which they had no immunity. In 1517, the Spanish started importing slaves from Africa to replace the Arawaks. But under Spanish rule, Jamaica suffered increasingly from neglect, internal strife, and raids by pirates and European forces jealous of Spain's powerful grip on the Caribbean.

Enter the British

A large expeditionary fleet, sent from Britain by Oliver Cromwell, was defeated in an attack on Hispaniola (now Haiti and the Dominican Republic) – so they decided to go on to the weaker island of Jamaica. In 1655, the British sailed into what is now Kingston

Harbour and marched to Spanish Town. But the Spaniards had fled to the north coast and on to Cuba – taking with them their valuables and freeing their slaves.

The retreating Spanish left arms with their slaves, instructing them to harass the invaders until they had an opportunity to return. The slaves took to the most inaccessible highlands and from these wild areas made surprise attacks on the British for over a century. These people became known as the Maroons (from the Spanish *cimarrón*, meaning 'wild' or 'living on peaks').

A Spanish attempt at recapturing Jamaica failed after a fierce battle at Rio Nuevo, on the north coast, in 1658. Finally, the island was ceded to the British crown under the Treaty of Madrid (1670). There is little evidence today of this period of Spanish rule – except various names.

Pirates and Privateers

Under the British, Jamaica saw increasing prosperity – despite tempestuous times – and became one of the most valuable colonies of the Caribbean. In the early days, the buccaneers brought riches to the island. They had originally been a motley crew of renegades who hunted pigs and cattle in the north of Hispaniola, and traded with passing ships. Their name comes from *boucan*, the wooden frame on which they cured the meat. The buccaneers banded together, and with captured Spanish ships and arms, began making raids further afield – and plundered more glittering prizes than pork. Some of their terrorist activities were made legal by letters of marque, issued by the English and French to encourage harassment of the Spanish by privateers. Port Royal (by Kingston Harbour) became the buccaneers' home base, where they traded and spent their booty – carousing and debauchery were the order of the day (and night). Their lair became known as 'the richest, wickedest, city in the world'. Henry Morgan, a ruthless and resourceful Welshman, was a renowned leader among the 'Brethren of the Coast'. After a rumbustious buccaneering career, he was

tried for piracy in London, aquitted on patriotic grounds and then knighted. He returned to Jamaica to become governor – and, with amazing audacity, tried to crack down on buccaneering! When he died in 1688, he was buried with state honours in his beloved Port Royal.

The demise of this buccaneering capital came four years later, when it was toppled into the sea by an earthquake. Throughout the 18th century there was conflict in the Caribbean between the British, Spanish and French, and pirates continued to plague ships and coastal areas. Among these colourful characters was 'Calico Jack' Rackham, who liked to wear calico underwear; after being captured in Negril harbour, two of his toughest crew members were found to be women. As protection against such incursions, the British built many forts. Port Royal became an important naval station, and it was here at Fort Charles that a young Horatio Nelson was given a command post at the end of the 18th century.

Maroons in the Mountains

In the late 17th and early 18th centuries, the British were also beset by internal attacks from the Maroons. Concentrated in the remote areas of Cockpit Country and the northeastern mountains (where their descendants still live today), they remained fiercely independent and continued to beleaguer the British empire-builders. They swept down from the hills at night to set fire to fields and steal stock. Their numbers were swelled by Breakaways, slaves who escaped the plantations. In 1690, forces of rebel slaves, led by a general called Cudjoe, joined with the Maroons to launch the First Maroon War (the Second War was in 1795). Skilled at using the forests and caves of their rugged home terrain to avoid capture by the better-armed troops, the Maroons fought a hard guerilla war. The Windward Maroons in the Blue Mountains were led by the indomitable and courageous warrior priestess, Queen Nanny – reputed to repel enemy fire with her backside! But after Nanny Town was

BACKGROUND

destroyed, the British began to get the upper hand. Finally, the Cockpit Maroons agreed peace terms in 1739, and the Blue Mountain Maroons a year later. This treaty guaranteed them a considerable measure of self-government, which they still enjoy today. And the 'Right Excellent Nanny' and Cudjoe have entered the realms of national legend.

Slaves and Sugar

Jamaica's sugar plantations grew and multiplied – along with the slave trade. The huge sugar estates reached their heyday in the 18th century – the island had 57 in 1673, which leapt to 430 by 1739 – bringing great prosperity and power to their owners. Rich planters built elegant Great Houses and enjoyed a life of lavish luxury (often in Europe), while their slaves lived a miserable existence of forced labour. By 1800 there were 300,000 slaves, 15 times the number of whites on the island.

The slaves were ruled with a rod of iron, since their despised white masters constantly feared uprisings in which they might be murdered or the plantation destroyed. In 1760, a slave called Tacky led a serious revolt in the Port Maria area on the north coast; and Tacky's Rebellion sparked off uprisings in other areas. After several months of terrible bloodshed, the revolts were stamped out.

Political reforms in Britain led to the abolition of the slave trade in 1807. But Jamaica's ruling class fiercely opposed the emancipation of slaves – and the Nonconformist missionaries who supported the slaves' cause. The unrest culminated in another bloody rebellion in 1831, instigated by 'Daddy' Sam Sharpe, a Baptist preacher; the square in Montego Bay where he was hanged now bears his name. It signalled the end of slavery, and full emancipation was granted by the British Parliament in 1838.

However, having left the estates, the freed slaves lived in abject poverty. Baptist preacher Paul Bogle led a protest that became the Morant Bay Rebellion, in 1865. It was put down with great severity – more than

Left: the 1865 rebellion

400 protesters were shot or hanged (including Bogle), hundreds flogged and thousands of homes destroyed. Sam Sharpe and Paul Bogle have both become national heroes. Many of the Great Houses on the plantations were burnt during the slave rebellions. And after the abolition of slavery, the plantations and sugar production fell into decline – despite efforts to bring in workers from elsewhere. But at the end of the 19th century, bananas began to boom.

Independence

Under the new Crown Colony system of government, Jamaica saw some reforms and improvements by the turn of the century, but it was hit hard by the depression in the 1930s. Discontent grew due to many factors – growing unemployment, economic difficulties such as the devastation of the banana industry through disease, the fact that most blacks still had no vote – and finally erupted in widespread rioting and violence in 1938. Two important figures emerged at this time: Alexander Bustamante, a Trade Unionist who later formed the Labour Party; and Norman Manley, a leading barrister who founded the People's National Party. Their campaigns for better wages and working conditions, along with political reform, paved the way for the new constitution of 1944, based on universal adult suffrage. Complete political independence for Jamaica came on 6 August 1962 – as a self-governing member of the British Commonwealth.

Since then, Jamaica has maintained a strong democratic spirit, although politics arouse volatile and stormy passions.

The People

Jamaica has about two and a half million inhabitants. A third of them live in Kingston, while 60 per cent live in rural areas. The vast majority are black, descendants of the slaves shipped over from many different tribes in Africa. Up to 1838, Britain and Africa had been the ancestral countries of nearly all the island's inhabitants – apart from a few Spanish and Portuguese Jews. Then after the abolition of slavery, workers and servants

BACKGROUND

were recruited from India, China, even Germany, Scotland and Ireland; Syrians (from what is now Lebanon) arrived as salesmen. Their descendants have added to the ethnic mix today, in which the percentage of white Jamaicans is very small. But these minority groups have influence that far outweighs their numbers; and most of the wealthy people in Jamaica are white. Mixed marriage has resulted in the exciting range of skin tones and facial features to be seen in Jamaica; but this is still a stratified society.

Slavery has had an indelible effect on Jamaica's heritage – apart from bringing in the majority race. For example, slaves were encouraged to have children but not allowed long-term relationships, and this is still reflected in the pattern of family life today. Many women have several children before (if ever) getting married, and the children are looked after by female members of the family – who are characteristically strong and independent. (But that is not to say that men don't have very sexist attitudes to women.) Under British rule, the mulattos were given more favours and power than their black half-brothers, creating a hierarchy that still survives.

Religion has always played an important role here – perhaps as a source of hope in a hard life – from the Catholic priests who wanted to save the souls of the Arawaks and Africans, to the uniquely Jamaican Rastafarians. As with other aspects of Jamaican culture that have combined different ethnic influences, Christianity has been blended with African beliefs and rituals. Cults still practised by a few – or which have contributed elements to Afro-Christian sects – include *Obeah* and *Myal* (sorcery), and related cults *Kumina* (meaning to move with rhythm) and *Bongo*, which believe in the power of *duppies* (ghosts), and use drumming, dancing and spiritual trances. The Baptist missionaries were important in the abolitionist movement at the beginning of the 19th century, and so Nonconformist religions have had more success in introducing Christian practices. African beliefs merged with the Baptist faith

Right: jerk pork and coconut water

at that time to produce the Revival movement, with sects like *Pocomania*. Now the most popular denominations are Anglican, Baptist and Methodist – but there is a variety of other faiths and sects to be found. American-style fundamentalists have grown in popularity in recent years, with plenty of singing and hand-clapping.

Rastafarianism has had a profound effect on Jamaican society, both on the island and abroad. It was founded by Marcus Garvey, who set up the Universal Negro Improvement Association in 1914, awakening black consciousness and pride, and advocating the 'back to Africa' cause. When Ras Tafari was crowned Emperor of Ethiopia, taking the name Haile Selassie ('Might of the Trinity'), he was regarded as the Black Messiah. And Ethiopia was the promised land to which the lost black tribe of Israel would one day return. In the depressed 1930s, the poor folk of Jamaica were ready for a new religion of hope. Its adherents live according to a code which includes living in harmony with nature and *Jah* (God), believing everyone is equal, opposing greed and exploitation, desiring no more than the essentials of life, not eating meat and shellfish (or drinking alcohol), Bible reading and smoking the sacramental herb *ganja*.

Rastas do not cut their hair, and their distinctive dreadlocks are inspired by the sacred symbol of the lion (taken from one of Selassie's titles, Lion of Judah), as well as African hairstyles. The red, green and gold colours, which you see everywhere, come from the Ethiopian flag. Some of their beliefs may seem confusing and illogical (this applies to most religions), but true Rastas are peaceful, honest, spiritual people. And out of their non-violent protest against oppression grew reggae. The development of this universally popular Jamaican music has been inextricably linked with Rastafarianism – and has produced many stars, notably Bob Marley and the Wailers. Some of the trappings of the Rasta movement – especially the hairstyle – have been taken up by people jumping on the bandwagon. But

BACKGROUND

Rastafarianism has been responsible for giving many Jamaicans an identity of their own and a pride in their nationality, and in being black.

Music – along with singing and dancing – has always been close to the heart of Jamaicans. Its roots lie in the African traditions the slaves brought with them. Other musical influences were absorbed to produce a sound uniquely Jamaican. In the 1960s, the funky beat of ska and the more languid rock-steady achieved universal popularity. The heavy bass rhythms of reggae, often with words of protest, were born in the late 1960s. It soon made an international impact and is still popular, having created a booming music industry in Jamaica.

Artistic talent blooms in Jamaica. The love of colour and drama can be seen reflected in everyday life; a simple bar will have bright designs painted on the walls, while a game of dominoes can be a performance art.

Jamaicans are a proud people – which can be seen in the way they talk (as equals) and walk (dignified, often strutting). Those you meet – especially in rural areas – are generally welcoming, open and down-to-earth. However, since visitors seem so well-off compared to most locals (and they certainly see it that way), you will be expected to spend money freely and hand out tips at the slightest opportunity. And if you want to take a photo of local people, you'll probably be asked for a tip. It's mainly a symptom of the contrast between rich and poor, and much less likely to be encountered in the southern or inland areas where the smart hotels and tourists have not yet reached.

If you are interested in really understanding the Jamaican way of life and meeting the locals, find out about the Jamaica Tourist Board's 'Meet The People' scheme. Or contact Diana McIntyre-Pike, at the Astra Hotel in Mandeville, who energetically promotes 'community tourism' (especially around the south, but she is a fount of knowledge and useful advice about all Jamaica). It could help you make the most of your visit.

NORTHWEST AND WEST

Doctor's Cave Beach, Montego Bay

Lying in the county of Cornwall, this area covers the parishes of St James, Trelawny, Hanover and the north of Westmoreland. It boasts two of the island's three main resorts, namely Montego Bay and Negril, where most of Jamaica's visitors stay (along with Ocho Rios further east, see page 38) – usually flown in on the big jets landing at Montego Bay's international airport.

The narrow coastal plain along the north has a backdrop of wooded hills, in places (west of Montego Bay) rising quite abruptly from the main road that hugs the coast. Generally, the scenery along the coast is less interesting than inland, where it becomes much more dramatic. The hillsides around Montego Bay are more jungly than further west, and rise to 1,850 feet (564m) just a few miles inland of the resort. To the southeast are the mysterious highlands of Cockpit Country.

Hanover, to the west, is also mountainous inland, with an unspoilt rocky coastline. Some of its bays and coves have strips of silvery sand, but the beaches are less good as you put Montego Bay behind you – the rocks and coral reefs in shallow seas make bathing difficult. The best beach is on the western tip of the island at Negril: seven miles (11km) of shimmering sand and turquoise sea, backed by a resort development.

Hotels spread along the coast either side of the town of Montego Bay, behind pretty sandy beaches. There are several old plantation Great Houses in this area which you can visit.

Parts of the coast are quite undeveloped, especially around Hanover, where the charming old town of Lucea is worth a visit. The main road along the coast heading east from Montego Bay is less attractive and busier. But on this stretch is another unspoilt old town, Falmouth.

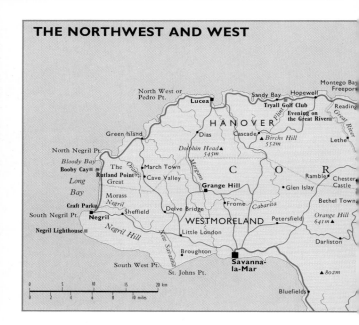

THE NORTHWEST AND WEST

WHAT TO SEE

◆◆
MONTEGO BAY

MoBay, as it is affectionately known, is Jamaica's second (and only) 'city' after Kingston. Accurately described as 'the gulf of good weather' by Columbus, in the Spanish era it was used for shipping pig lard, *manteca*, from which its name probably originates. Then it became an important sugar and banana port. Now life revolves around its major industry: tourism. It is Jamaica's tourist capital, and one of the most popular resorts in the Caribbean. Here there are top-notch hotels and sports galore – but not a lot of

authentic Jamaican atmosphere, except along the down-beat downtown back streets and street corners. The main street through the centre of town is St James Street, which leads to the **Sam Sharpe Square** roundabout. In one corner of the square is **The Cage**, once used to imprison runaway slaves: the group of bronze statues outside includes Sam Sharpe, the preacher who led the 1831 slave rebellion. A few streets east on Union Street is another reminder of the days of slavery, the crumbling stone **Slave Ring**, reputed to have been a slave market and then used for cockfighting. Two fine merchants' houses are worth a

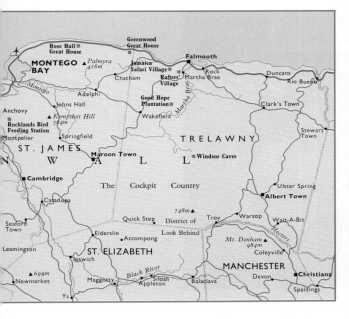

visit and are now restaurants: **The Georgian House** (on the corner of Union and Orange streets; it also has an art gallery) and the renowned **Town House** (on Church Street). **St James Parish Church**, sitting opposite the Town House, dates from 1775 (rebuilt after the 1957 earthquake); it is well worth a look as a reflection of a bygone era of affluence and elegance. Just northwest of the square, opposite Walter Fletcher Beach, are the remains of **Port Montego** with three cannons pointing out over the harbour. The wharves by **Harbour Street**, west of Sam Sharpe Square, are a hive of activity

when a fishing boat lands its catch. Nearby is the **Craft Market**, where tourists barter for souvenirs. Just to the south, off the main thoroughfare of Barnett Street, is the **Fustic Street Market** – full of hustle and bustle in real Jamaican style, especially on Fridays and Saturdays. Behind the main roads in the centre are narrow streets, often scruffy but equally colourful.

Montego Bay Freeport lies to the southwest of the town centre. This is also the location for the new cruise ship wharf, the ultra-smart Montego Bay Yacht Club and docks, and a large duty-free shopping centre. MoBay has recently opened its upgraded cruise

Jah David, a Crafts Marketeer

ship wharf to compete with Ocho Rios.

There are three main town beaches, all public, which charge a small entrance fee and provide a variety of facilities, from changing rooms to sports. **Walter Fletcher Beach** and its complex of facilities lies nearest the centre – and beside it is a small stretch of sand where you can bathe free. Just north of here is MoBay's famous **Doctor's Cave Beach**, popular since the 1920s. An attractive beach, like MoBay's others it has fine white sand, is deep enough for swimming and sheltered by the bay. Further up the road is **Cornwall Beach**, the smallest but also popular; the complex of facilities behind it includes the local Tourist Board office.

Accommodation

MoBay has a very wide range of accommodation from some of the smartest hotels in the Caribbean to simple guest houses. Most of the more moderately-priced accommodation is in town, particularly along the roads behind the beaches. The large and more up-market hotels are scattered along the coastal strip either side of the resort – especially to the east – behind private beaches.

There are three top hotels, which have rooms as well as villas set in beautiful estates by the coast – where very high prices will provide the class and sophistication to match. **Round Hill** (tel: 952 5150) is secluded on a lush peninsula 10 miles (16km) west of MoBay. It is a charming hotel, with an exclusive understated elegance in tasteful plantation-house and ethnic styles. The main buildings at **Tryall Golf, Tennis and Beach Club** (tel: 952 5110) which lies a few miles west of Round Hill are in an 18th-century Great House, sparkling white and beautifully furnished. On the coast east of MoBay is the extensive **Half Moon Golf, Tennis and Beach Club** (tel: 953 2211); eminently elegant, luxurious and stylish, it also has a very good restaurant and a golf course. Also on the coast east of the resort is the large, efficient, American-style, high-rise **Wyndham Rose Hall Beach Hotel** (tel: 953 2650), which has a golf course. Closer to MoBay on this stretch of coast is **Sandals Royal Caribbean** (tel: 953 2111), and near the airport its sister hotel, **Sandals Montego Bay** (tel: 952 5510); these are all-inclusive resort hotels for couples only, where everything from sports to drinks and tips is included in the price, and the accent is on fun and organised activity. A moderately-priced hotel, which has a great deal of character, is the small **Richmond Hill Inn** (tel: 952 3859), perched on a quiet hill above the resort with superb views; in an 18th-century Great House, it has a smart, old-fashioned style. In a similar price range are two comfortable hotels with attractive features, lying on the other side of the road running behind the main town beaches: **Doctor's Cave** (tel: 952 4355) and **Fantasy Resort** (tel: 952 4150), which both have good facilities including a pool. **Toby Inn** (tel: 952 4370) is a neat, intimate hotel next to the Fantasy, charging reasonable rates, with a pool set in gardens. Just past Rock is the

modern seven-storey **Trelawny Beach** hotel (tel: 954 2450), which also has cottage units set in gardens; prices are very reasonable and all-inclusive, with lots of sports and entertainment, and it is good for families in that it offers special facilities for children. For the budget-conscious, **Chalet Caribe** (tel: 952 1364/5) is a small hotel on the coast just west of Montego Bay (with a pool and beach). There's also **La Mirage** (tel: 952 4435), a modern little hotel, with a pool in its gardens and great views. Almost next door is the **Chatwick Gardens** (tel: 952 2147), charging even lower rates; it also has a pool. Among MoBay's guest houses are the **Seville Guest House Villas and Apartments** (tel: 952 3347) and homely **Ocean View Guest House** (tel: 952 2662), both down the road from the airport.

Nightlife and Entertainment
There is no lack of choice if you are looking for organised trips – full details can be

Tryall Golf Club, near Round Hill

NORTHWEST AND WEST

obtained from your hotel or local Tourist Board office. One of the most popular is the **Appleton Estate Express**, a jolly train trip (with an open bar) that stops at Catadupa, a village on the edge of Cockpit Country – where you can be measured up for a shirt or dress which you collect on the way back – and travels on to the Appleton Rum distillery, south of Cockpit Country, where there is a guided tour and buffet lunch; it also stops for a visit to the Ipswich Caves (see page 33). The **Governor's Coach Tour** (or Catadupa Choo Choo) offers much the same trip, with lunch at Maggotty, a pretty little riverside village near Appleton.

The **Hilton High Day Tour** passes through beautiful mountain countryside inland for Jamaican breakfast and lunch at the Hilton Plantation House, where you can go up in a hot-air balloon, walk to Seaford Town (see page 36) or go horse-riding.

There are many different boat cruises offered: for instance, on the old wooden sailing boat, the *Calico*, or a large metal catamaran, the *Bamboo Prince*. These trips include drinks, lunch, snorkelling, or visits along the coast, such as to Negril; there are also sunset cruises or night-time glass-bottomed boat trips.

Organised trips are available to many of the sights listed below in **What Else To See In The Northwest** and other areas on the island.

A popular night-time excursion is **An Evening on the Great River** (to the west of MoBay), with a ride in a fishing canoe up the torch-lit-river – and plenty of drinks – then a stop for a Jamaican barbecue, a 'native' show and dancing to live music. The **Cornwall Beach Party** has a barbecue and evening of reggae under the stars; parties are also held at Walter Fletcher Beach. Rose Hall offers a **Spooky Candlelight Tour** with dinner and music.

There is a variety of action after dark in MoBay; the major hotels have nightly entertainment. Among the discos are **Connections** at the Fantasy Resort Hotel, **Pier 1 On The Waterfront** (Howard Cooke Boulevard), and **The Cave** at the Seawind Beach Resort hotel (by Montego Bay Freeport). Reggae fans should try **Sir Winston's Reggae Club** on the Gloucester Avenue. A mellower pace is set at the Doctor's Cave Beach Hotel's piano bar.

In July/August, you can hear reggae galore among the crowds thronging the **Reggae Sunsplash Festival**, held at the Bob Marley Performing Centre (Tourist Boards have exact dates each year).

Restaurants

There are plenty of restaurants, from those in swank hotels to basic snack bars and stalls, from US-style fast food to Chinese. Many restaurants offer free transport to and from hotels. Several of the hotels have good restaurants – including the

Richmond Hill Inn
(tel: 952 3859), with a romantic view of the twinkling lights of MoBay from its open-air terrace. The **Town House**, Church Street (tel: 952 2660) is one of the best-known restaurants, lying near the centre in an 18th-century merchant's house with a pretty flowery courtyard; it serves a menu of delicious fresh fish and Jamaican or American-style dishes – tasty food in an attractive ambience.
Marguerite's By The Sea, Gloucester Avenue, (tel: 952 4777) is a pretty place with a terrace right on the sea, overlooking the bay – and it serves good fish.

Shopping
MoBay has lots of opportunities for shopping. Generally items are cheaper here in downtown shops than along the tourist strip, or at hotel shops out of town. There are several modern shopping plazas, with duty-free shops selling imported watches, jewellery, cameras, electrical goods, crystal, china and perfume – for example, the **City Centre Building** near Sam Sharpe Square, **St James Place Shopping Arcade** by Cornwall Beach, and **Montego Bay Freeport Shopping Centre**. Other places include the **Overton Shopping Plaza**, up the hill on Union Street, and the **Beachview Shopping Plaza** on Gloucester Avenue behind the beaches.
The **Crafts Market**, near the centre, is the place to go to bargain for locally-made straw

Music on the streets, Montego Bay

hats, baskets and mats, wooden carvings, T-shirts, tie-dyed clothes and shell jewellery. Good quality Jamaican paintings and carvings can be found at **Liz DeLisser's Gallery of West Indian Art**, at 1 Orange Lane, and wooden items at the **Native Shop** in the Beachview Shopping Plaza.
For an extravaganza of everyday goods, including food, visit the **Fustic Street Market**.
There are organised shopping excursions into MoBay from some hotels.

Sports
No problem, here, either – whatever you enjoy. Jamaica was made for watersports, but from golf to horse-riding, you will find your sport here. Your hotel or the Tourist Board will provide up-to-the minute information.

◆◆◆
NEGRIL

This is a very rapidly expanding resort. Originally named Negrillo by the Spanish, its harbour occasionally sheltered the English fleet and pirates in the 18th century – this is where the infamous 'Calico Jack' Rackham was captured. Until 25 years ago, Negril was no more than a small, isolated fishing village, without phones or electricity. Then it became an escapists' haven for Rastas and itinerant hippies, who lived the natural life in huts and tents along the beach. Word got around about its unspoilt beauty, but it was only 10 years ago that the explosion of tourist development started.

Guiding light: Negril lighthouse

Negril's major attraction is its superb, seven-mile (11km) stretch of luminous white sands. The resort hugs the coastline, running either side of the road the whole length of the beach and along the cliffs to the south. It is very different to Montego Bay and Ocho Rios in that it has not developed around a town; it is purely a resort and feels as if it has no life of its own apart from tourism. There is scant evidence of the original settlement which has been swamped by new development. Anyone who knew and loved Negril 20 years ago must regret the transformation; but new visitors will love its beautiful setting. Despite the commercialisation, it is an appealing resort – no buildings rise much higher than the palm trees and many are designed in attractive 'ethnic' styles, surrounded by gardens.

Negril has a light-hearted, colourful atmosphere, with the emphasis on relaxation and pleasures of the flesh. Its reputation as a hedonistic holiday paradise lures increasing numbers of visitors from all walks of life. More than anywhere else on the island, you can do as you please here – including sunbathe nude or party all night.

The centre of Negril lies at the junction of the beach road and the cliff-top road, where the road from the south coast enters the resort. Near the roundabout is a central square with shopping complexes (including the Tourist Board office), and the **Negril Craft Park** which is set behind the beach. Here also, the Negril River runs into the sea; boats are moored along it, and nearby are jetties from where sunset cruises and other boat trips leave.

The northern section of the resort lies along Norman Manley Boulevard, behind Long Bay, up to Negril Harbour in the north. This has a pretty crescent of sand, set beneath tree-covered cliffs, known as **Bloody Bay**, a name dating from the days when whalers cleaned their catch here – now it is better known as a nude beach. Offshore you can see **Booby Cay**, a coral islet which can be reached by boat. Negril's airstrip and the Rutland Point craft market are set on the inland side of the road, near the points which divide Bloody Bay from Long Bay.

Long Bay is the pride of Negril: miles of dazzling white soft sand bathed in the translucent, aquamarine sea, which is calm and perfect for swimming, protected by a coral reef further out. A beachcomber's delight – the beach is so long it does not feel crowded, although there is plenty of action here. Upper parts of the beach in front of hotels are often private, with beach beds, palm-thatched shelters and hammocks, barbecue huts and bars. There are lots of local people selling T-shirts, wood carving, straw hats, shells, reggae tapes, snacks and sometimes *ganja*. Masses of

watersports and excursions are available, from waterskiing to parasailing, snorkelling, diving, glass-bottomed boat trips and windsurfing. The most peaceful parts of the beach are towards the north. On the east side of the beach road is a flat landscape of low bush and swamp – the **Great Morass**. These peaty wetlands are an area of National Park, where many interesting birds and plants may be found.

The southern section of Negril lies along the narrow, winding West End road which skirts the cliffs and rocky coves around to **Negril Lighthouse** – a 100 foot (30m) landmark that's guided sailors round the coast for 100 years. Some of the cheaper accommodation lies along here, including palm-thatched huts perched on the cliff tops. This is the most relaxed, easy-going end of the resort; little sophistication here, but plenty of life. It attracts the young crowd and still has colourful reminders of its past popularity with Rastas (such as the Lion Café, Jah-Bull's Ital Shop, Dread Fruit Stand). Views of the sunsets are especially good from this southwesterly point, and **Rick's Café** is the most popular spot to catch this spectacular natural show, as well as to eat fish and watch daring young divers plunge into the waves from the cliffs.

Since Negril is one long development that sticks to the beach and cliffs, you can quickly leave the resort behind to explore the quiet surrounding countryside.

Accommodation

Almost all the accommodation is spread along the coast. The larger, more up-market hotels are towards the north end of Long Bay, while the cheaper (and often more characterful) accommodation tends to be at the southern end of the resort, mainly along the West End road but also inland. You can find a wide range, from classy hotels to tiny cabins or camping, including a variety of self-catering villas and rustic chalets. Many hotels have rooms in small blocks or cottages, too, and some offer accommodation with self-catering facilities as well as a restaurant.

The most attractive of the large, all-inclusive hotels to the north of Long Bay is **Swept Away** (tel: 957 4061), which has well-designed cottages secluded in 10 acres (4 hectares) of gardens beside the beach. In a similar price bracket is **Sandals Negril** (tel: 957 4216), which is in much the same vein as other Sandals hotels – such as the one at Montego Bay. Those in search of a carefree hotbed of adult holiday fun and games, rather than a haven, should try the neighbouring **Hedonism II** (tel: 957 4201). Next to it lies the sophisticated and slightly pricier **Grand Lido** (tel: 957 4010), also all-inclusive but much more formal than the other Negril hotels. All have extensive facilities.

Lying beside Long Bay beach, on Norman Manley Boulevard, are several comfortable, moderately-priced hotels

offering a variety of amenities. The rather Spanish-style **Charela Inn** (tel: 957 4277) has a personal atmosphere; the **Negril Tree House** (tel: 957 4386) is an appealing ethnic style building, it also has cottages with kitchenettes; the **Negril Gardens** (tel: 957 4408) has a pretty pink and white colour scheme. A bit more expensive is the quiet, small and neat **Seasplash** (tel: 957 4041).

Secluded amongst the trees, north of the beach and the airstrip (on the inland side of the road) are the reasonably-priced **Negril Cabins** (tel: 957 4350), wooden chalets on stilts and furnished. They have no cooking facilities, but there is a restaurant. Straightforward self-catering cottages offering homely comfort at reasonable rates include **Yellow Bird Sea-Tel** (tel: 957 4252) and **Crystal Waters** (tel: 957 4284), both conveniently located on the beach. For budget self-catering in the same area, try **The Golden Sunset** (tel: 957 4241), for either rooms or cottages – it has a good restaurant by the beach. The **Negril Yoga Centre** (tel: 957 4397) also has low-priced accommodation in a few rustic cabins and cottages set in gardens near the centre, across the road from the beach (some have cooking facilities). The moderately-priced **Rockhouse** (tel: 957 4373) has romantic little palm-thatched, wooden rondavel cottages clustered on the cliff-tops; they have hot plates for cooking but

A romantic setting at Rockhouse

there is also a restaurant – there is no pool but steps lead down to the clear coves below. In a similar price range is the **Rock Cliff** (tel: 957 4331), a comfortable, friendly hotel on the cliffs with a pool. On the inland side of West End road is a lively, slightly cheaper hotel: **Thrills** (tel: 957 4390). Ethnic Negril can be found at reasonable prices at **Awee Maway** (no telephone; book in Miami (305) 2555411). The cottages in gardens on the cliffs feature hammocks, waterbeds, sunken showers, and there is a thatched bamboo restaurant. Alternatively, nearby **Xtabi** (tel: 957 4336) is a lovely retreat, with a cliff-top restaurant.

Low rates and good value can be found at two properties inland of West End road and therefore some way from the beach. The attractive **Summerset Village** (tel: 957 4409) has a variety of charming villas (offering rooms or self-catering) set in gardens with a pool and restaurant.

Next to it is the rustic, peaceful **Addis Kokeb Guest House and Cottages** (tel: 957 4485); self-catering is available.

Nightlife and Entertainment

There is a good choice of organised excursions (by coach, boat or horse), to see some of the scenic spots around Negril as well as elsewhere on the island. These include trips that start in Montego Bay, like the **Appleton Estate Express, An Evening on the Great River** or touring by small airplane (see page 24).

Information on these tours can be obtained from hotels, concession booths on the beach or the local Tourist Board.

The pace of Negril hots up after the sun goes down. There are a few organised evening excursions including a sunset party cruise, where you can dance to live reggae, see a folk show or enjoy a barbecue. Regular live reggae shows are put on at the **Negril Tree House**, **Samsara**, **Summerset Village** or **Thrills**. The **Charela Inn** has a folklore show. And there are hotel discos, for instance, at the **Negril Gardens**, **Hedonism II** and the up-market, expensive **Grand Lido** (but visitors must buy a meal at the latter two all-inclusive hotels). Discos in the centre of town include the funky **Compulsion** at the Plaza de Negril, and **Close Encounters** at Kings Plaza. The hot favourite for live reggae is **Kaiser's Café**, a short distance down West End road, with top performers on Wednesdays and Fridays; the restaurant is open nightly, serving seafood and local dishes. Another haunt of reggae fans is **De Buss**, by the beach on Norman Manley Boulevard (you can't miss the painted double-decker bus), which puts on live shows once or twice a week including Sundays. **Rick's Café** (see **Restaurants**) sometimes has live music.

There is good music every night at **Mandela's Green Entertainment Centre** (see **Restaurants**), which is in Green Island north of Negril.

So much for the organised nightlife. But in Negril, there is always the chance of an impromptu beach party, which can be the most fun of all.

Restaurants

Take pot luck and you will find all sorts of cafés and palm-thatched beach bars serving tasty snacks – there is even a 24-hour restaurant along West End road. An atmospheric and busy place to eat is **Rick's Café**, Lighthouse Road (tel: 957 4335), perched on the cliffs around the West End point. The blackboard menu includes a variety of fish dishes (not cheap), and you exchange money for beads to buy drinks at the bar.

Lots of the hotels have good restaurants, such as the **Charela Inn** (tel: 957 4277), which serves Jamaican and French dishes either on the patio by the beach or in the smart dining room. A little further north on Long Bay is **Cosmo's Seafood Restaurant and Bar** (tel: 957 4330), in a large wood and bamboo barn on the beach, open to the breezes, with big wooden tables and benches; it offers local fare at very reasonable prices in a relaxed atmosphere – a favourite with Jamaicans and tourists alike.

Among the little Rasta joints in the resort, try **Desi Dread's Ital Food**, which is a tiny wooden shack on the beach at the Negril Craft Park. Ital means natural, and that goes for everything – from the way they cook the vegetarian dishes, like delicious stews or spicy patties, to the wooden eating utensils. There is also an interesting range of fresh juices.

Several miles north of Negril, at a fishing village called Green Island, is **Mandela's Green Entertainment Centre**. Recently-opened, there is a palm-thatched upper floor giving lovely views over the bay; it serves good Jamaican food at low prices. A peaceful spot during the day, at night it puts on excellent shows, such as live reggae music.

Shopping

Negril is not the best resort for shopping, being much more limited than the towns of Montego Bay or Ocho Rios. But there are plenty of craft and souvenir stalls along the beach and roadside. The main craft market is the lively **Negril Craft Park**, behind the beach at its southern end (near the centre of the resort). Here there are lots of little wooden and concrete huts, selling tie-dyed clothes, hammocks, coral and shell jewellery, as well as T-shirts and fruit. The smaller **Rutland Point Craft Market** lies near the airstrip to the north of the resort.

The two main shopping complexes, near the central roundabout, are **Adrija Plaza** and **Plaza de Negril**, where there are a couple of shops selling duty-free goods; a short way down the West End road are **Kings Plaza** and the new **Sunshine Village**. These plazas

Jahbah's Health Food, Negril

are the place to come if you are looking for banks, supermarkets, pharmacies, a doctor, car rental or tourist information.

For local art try **Gallery Hoffstead II** at Plaza de Negril (there is also a branch in the little town of Lucea, see page 35), or the **Patrick Weise Studio Gallery** and **Geraldine Robins**, which are both along West End road and also sell handpainted clothes.

Sports

For those requiring more activity than just reclining on the beach, Negril has a wealth of watersports – offered by the larger hotels or several independent companies (the Tourist Board has an approved list). Almost any watersport you've ever wanted to try is available here, as Negril is the perfect location.

The larger hotels have various other sporting facilities, like tennis, squash and gyms. Some allow visitors to pay to use them – such as the **Swept Away Sport Complex**, which has an extensive range. The **Negril Yoga Centre** offers yoga classes.

WHAT ELSE TO SEE IN THE NORTHWEST AND WEST

Calm and clear: Great River

◆◆◆
COCKPIT COUNTRY

This haunting highland wilderness lies inland, southeast of Montego Bay, and rises to almost 2,500 feet (762m). The pockmarked *karst* plateau – with its craggy peaks, caverns, underground tunnels and streams, fissures and sinkholes, covered in verdant vegetation – is best known as being the home territory of the Maroons. Various evocative names in this land of 'Me No Sen, You No Come', are reminders of the time when the British rode back-to-back in pairs on one horse to try and avoid ambush: such as the District of Look Behind, Wait-A-Bit, and Quick Step. Remote villages are scattered around its fringes, reached by narrow, winding, rough roads – full of pot holes – and offering some breathtaking views of the steep, forested slopes. But not even rough tracks reach into its rugged, untouched heart; and much is inaccessible

except, perhaps, to intrepid explorers. The most popular way to catch a glimpse of its countryside is on the **Appleton Estate Express** train tour (see page 24), which travels from Montego Bay, skirting its western rim, to the Appleton Rum distillery (see page 24) south of Cockpit Country. High on the slopes of its southern side is the Maroon capital of Cockpit Country: a traditional village called **Accompong**. It is named after the brother of Cudjoe, who was leader of the First Maroon War. It was here, under a silk cotton tree, that they signed their peace treaty with the British.

On Cudjoe Day, 6 January, it becomes a place of pilgrimage for the Maroons, and is celebrated with much drumming and dancing. Normally this isolated village is a quiet place, its simple dwellings clinging to the jungly, rocky mountain sides – where the people are proud and friendly. Much of the pleasure of visiting it is for the drive there, through some spectacular scenery (from the north or the south, as it lies right in the interior of the island).

Southwest of Accompong are the **Ipswich Caves** visited en route on the Appleton Estate Express. Its impressive caverns have some striking stalactite and stalagmite formations. If you are interested in such geological wonders, the **Windsor Caves** are worth a visit – lying towards the uncharted depths of Cockpit Country on its northern flanks. These eerie caves are among the largest on the island, with splendid displays of stalactites and stalagmites.

◆◆
CROYDON PLANTATION

This working pineapple and coffee plantation is set amid majestic mountain scenery, surrounded by lush forested slopes and tranquil valleys – it lies about 20 miles (32km) south of Montego Bay, close to the western edge of Cockpit Country. A short guided walking tour explains some of its history, while showing modern cultivation and production techniques of various types of pineapple, other fruits, coffee and honey – you are able to taste some of the fruit. A popular way to see Croydon is on an organised excursion (from Montego Bay or Negril), which includes a barbecue lunch at the plantation.
Open: daily 10.00–13.30hrs.

◆◆
FALMOUTH

An appealing little town, on the flat coastal plain, 23 miles (37km) east of Montego Bay. It flourished as a sugar port from the late 18th century, but the port fell into disuse after the sugar industry declined and its harbour was unable to accommodate the new steam ships. Now rather scruffy, this almost adds to its unspoilt local character, with men mending nets by the sea and women selling wares on the street. It throngs with activity during the Wednesday market. You can see numerous examples of Georgian architecture along Market Street, just west of Water Square in the centre of town, including a **Methodist Manse** which was built in 1799 by the Barretts (the family of poet Elizabeth Barrett Browning), who helped plan the town. It has wrought-iron balconies and Adam-style doorways and friezes.

A couple of miles east, by Rock, is a phosphorescent lagoon that looks luminous at night. There is a very pleasant, inexpensive fish restaurant called **Glistening Waters** set directly on the deep bay, which also has a marina where you can take fishing charters or cruises. Nearby, on the main road, is **Caribatik**, a shop selling vibrant batik cotton or silk clothing and fabric, with a gallery of batik paintings (open Tuesday to Saturday, 10.00 to 15.00 hrs). Close by, up a track off the main road, are the ruins of a large, fortified house, **Stewart Castle**.

Greenwood recalls another age

♦♦
GREAT RIVER RAFTING

To appreciate the inland countryside at its tranquil best, a raft trip is highly recommended. This one starts high in the hills at the village of Lethe. The long bamboo rafts seat two people; you are punted downstream for about an hour, through gentle rapids, and shown points of interest on the way. Apart from the spectacular scenery, it can also give you a glimpse of typical local life along the banks – such as women washing clothes or children bathing. You can take a dip in the clear, green water, and stop at a riverside bar for a drink; there is also an optional visit to a fruit plantation. You disembark at a recreation area, where you can laze in a hammock with a drink or take a donkey ride. Rafts run daily, 09.00 to 16.00hrs.

♦♦
GREENWOOD GREAT HOUSE

Set on a hill above the coastal strip, up a steep rough road, this fine old plantation house is built of stone and wood, with a shingle roof, and is surrounded by very pretty gardens. It dates from 1790, built by the poet Elizabeth Barrett Browning's family, who were one of the largest landowners in Jamaica. Their property included 2,000 slaves. This estate extended 12 miles (19km) along the coast – of which it commands wonderful views from the white-painted upper veranda along the bank of the house. The elegant interior has many interesting and beautiful antiques – some owned by the Barretts, the rest collected by the present owners.

After the tour you can relax with a drink in the original kitchen which is now a bar. About 16 miles (25km) east of Montego Bay.
Open: daily 09.00–18.00hrs.

♦
JAMAICA SAFARI VILLAGE

This open-air park is set in a mangrove swamp just west of Falmouth. Crocodiles, snakes and birds may be seen in their natural habitat, as well as small enclosures with various unhappy-looking animals, like the lioness. There are boat trips and refreshment facilities. *Open*: daily 08.30–17.30hrs.

◆◆
LUCEA
Once a thriving sugar port, Lucea's harbour remains one of the best on the north coast; now it mainly ships bananas and molasses. Allspice, ginger and yams are also important local products – and fishing boats bring in their catches. On Saturdays, the town has a big, bustling market. Lucea has much unspoilt character, and it owes part of its charm to the old buildings along its narrow streets – including some stone and wood Georgian architecture and lots of appealing cream-painted clapboard houses with 'gingerbread' fretwork around the balconies. By the central square – named after Alexander Bustamante (Jamaica's first Prime Minister) who was born near Lucea – is the attractive 19th-century **Courthouse**. This cream wood building, with stone balustrades, has an unusual clock-tower supported by Corinthian-style columns, of which Lucea is very proud. On a peninsula just to the north of the town, overlooking Lucea's harbour, is the delapidated 18th-century **Fort Charlotte**, named after George III's queen. Near by, beside a big Catholic church, is the much more interesting **Hanover Museum**, set right by

the sea in the old British barracks. Very recently opened, and still expanding, it contains displays of historical artefacts, including Arawak Indian tools and pots and various pieces of old equipment and pictures. It has a restaurant and shop.
Open: daily 09.00–18.00hrs.
From Lucea, you can drive up into the mountains, to the south and southeast, for wonderful panoramas and complete peace. Lucea lies 28 miles (45km) west of Montego Bay.

◆◆
MARTHA BRAE RAFTING
The Martha Brae River was named after a mythical Arawak Indian girl with supernatural powers. The river flows into the phosphorescent lagoon near Falmouth, and the rafting trip starts at Rafters' Village three miles (5km) south. Here you will find a restaurant, bar, souvenir kiosks, swimming pool, supervised children's play area and a shady picnic area. The long bamboo raft glides down the meandering river, through low hills and lush green foliage, with only the 'splunk' of the rafter's pole in the sparkling green water to break the peace. The trip takes an hour and a half and is a lovely way to see some of the unspoilt countryside and the flora, including fringes of feathery bamboo, vine-tangled woods and banana plantations, as well as many colourful birds and butterflies. The rafts (which seat two people) run daily from 09.00 to 16.00hrs.

◆◆◆
ROCKLANDS BIRD FEEDING STATION

In the steep, forested highlands near Anchovy, nine miles (14km) south of Montego Bay, is a small property owned by Lisa Salmon – fondly known as 'the bird lady'. She set up her bird feeding station here in 1958. In the late afternoon she puts out food on the patio, and all sorts of native and migrating wild birds come to feed. The birds take seeds from your hand, and humming birds – like the delightful Doctor Bird – sip sugar-water from little bottles Miss Salmon gives you to hold.

Open: daily 15.15hrs to sunset (feeding starts between 15.30 and 16.00hrs) – children under four not admitted.

◆◆◆
ROSE HALL GREAT HOUSE

This grandest of Jamaica's Great Houses is also renowned for the haunting legend of the 'White Witch', Annie Palmer. It was built around 1770, then fell into ruin during the last century, but was restored to its former glory in the 1960s. The symmetrical façade is striking, with its Palladian portico and balustraded terrace reached by two flights of steps. Inside it is graced by rich woodwork, and the owners have tried to recreate the original elegance and splendour of an 18th-century colonial manor. It is full of fine antiques and art treasures, collected from around the world.

The infamous Annie Palmer was a former mistress of Rose Hall. Legend has it that she was practised in the art of Voodoo magic, and managed to kill off three husbands by poisoning, strangling and stabbing. She was also said to have taken slaves as lovers, murdering them when she got bored, and entertained herself by watching slaves being tortured. Finally, when the slave rebellion started in 1831, she was killed – one story claims it was by an African witch doctor whom she had seduced – and her ghost (*duppy*) is said to haunt Rose Hall. The guides here are very knowledgeable and bring the history alive. There is a small restaurant, Annie's Pub and gift shop. About 10 miles (16km) east of Montego Bay. *Open*: daily 09.00–18.00hrs.

◆
SEAFORD TOWN

Lying in the mountainous western interior, about 25 miles (40km) south of Montego Bay, this small place is best known for its community of German descendants. Peasant farmers from North Germany settled here in the mid-19th century to cultivate sugar and bananas. The fair-skinned, blue-eyed inhabitants have preserved little of their culture (bar their surnames) and speak no German. Sadly, they are an impoverished group – about the only poor whites living in Jamaica. There is a small historical museum, with a display of memorabilia, by the old Catholic church.

Open: Monday to Saturday 10.00–16.00hrs.

CENTRAL NORTH COAST

Peace and quiet in Ocho Rios

This area covers the northern part of the county of Middlesex, including the parishes of St Ann and St Mary. It is here that Ocho Rios lies – Jamaica's second most important resort – as well as the popular resort of Runaway Bay, west of Ocho Rios.

The busiest stretch of the main road along the coast is between Ocho Rios and Montego Bay, further west. Much of the scenery along this coastal strip is quite similar, with pastureland, low bush and trees. It rises quickly to verdant wooded hills and mountains inland, cut by the valleys of many rivers running into the sea. Close to the coast there are sugar cane, coconut, citrus and banana plantations – as well as trunks of palms that succumbed to a dreaded disease, leaving them bare and precarious. And, as always, there are goats nibbling the foliage beside the road.

As you go east, the landscapes become increasingly interesting along the coast, with steep hills ascending directly from the cliffs and coves, and more lush, jungly vegetation – especially after you enter St Mary, past Ocho Rios, where there is dramatic coastal scenery in places. There are some beautiful views over the coastline, and towards the east you begin to see the peaks of the Blue Mountains in the hazy distance. It is noticeably less touristy and quieter as Ocho Rios is left behind.

As in the northwest, although development is spreading on either side of the resorts along the coast, parts are still unspoilt (especially in St Mary). The best beaches in this area are around Ocho Rios – coves of sparkling white sands. The sandy bays around Runaway Bay are generally shallower and more rocky. St Mary's coastline tends to be rocky, with cliffs and beaches of grey shingly sand.

CENTRAL NORTH COAST

WHAT TO SEE

♦♦
OCHO RIOS
Jamaica's second tourist
mecca is said to derive its
name from the Spanish *Las
Chorreras* – referring to its
waterfalls, especially the
splendid **Dunn's River Falls**
west of the town (see page 50).
Whether the British misheard
(or couldn't count), it came to
be called Ocho Rios –
meaning 'eight rivers' – now
simply nicknamed Ochi by the
locals. Whereas other north
coast towns have declined
from busy ports into quiet
fishing villages, Ocho Rios has
done the reverse, thanks to its
development as a centre for
tourism and shipping bauxite.
In recent years, it has become
Jamaica's prime cruise ship
destination (although Montego
Bay is fighting back).
There are no historic
buildings, except the remains
of a late 17th-century **fort** with
a couple of cannons, by the
main road on the western edge
of town – lying next to a dusty
bauxite installation. Ochi
boasts a very attractive setting:
the centre lies behind Ocho
Rios Bay, whose clear
turquoise sea is bordered by a
crescent of white sand. It is
surrounded by a bowl of steep,
green hills, luxuriantly
covered in tropical vegetation.
As the continuous row of
shops, restaurants, car-rental
offices and other buildings
peter out, some of the larger
and most elegant hotels (and
grand villas) take over,
hugging the coast and hidden

in lush gardens. Here,
between the cliffs and rocky
points, which are thickly
fringed with foliage, small
strips of sand nestle in coves.
Ochi is full of fun – and
commercialisation. When a
cruise ship arrives in town, it
heaves with thronging tourists
and locals trying to tout for
business. But even when there
are no visiting cruise
passengers, the resort hums
with people and traffic. It is not
subtle about the fact that it is
very geared to visitors.
The area by Ocho Rios Bay is a
hub of activity. The high-rise
hotel blocks set around it are
landmarks as you enter the
resort. On the west side of the
bay, near the bauxite terminal,
is the cruise ship wharf. And
when a gleaming luxury liner

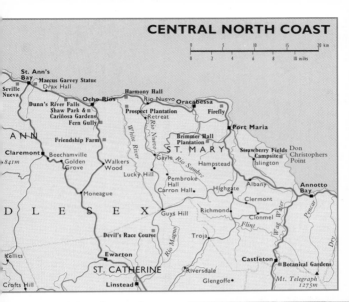

CENTRAL NORTH COAST

St. Ann's Bay · Marcus Garvey Statue · Drax Hall · Harmony Hall · Rio Nuevo · Oracabessa
Seville Nueva · Ocho Rios · Prospect Plantation · Firefly
Dunn's River Falls · Shaw Park & Cariñosa Gardens · Fern Gully · Retreat · Rio Nuevo · Port Maria
Brimmer Hall Plantation
A N N · Friendship Farm · ST. MARY · Strawberry Fields Campsite · Don Christophers Point
Claremont · Beechamville · Gayle · Rio Sambra · Hampstead · Islington
△ 841m · Golden Grove · Walkers Wood · Lucky Hill · Pembroke Hall · Carron Hall · Highgate · Albany · Annotto Bay
Moneague · Clermont · Clonmel
D L E S E X · Guys Hill · Richmond · Flint · Wag Water
Devil's Race Course · Rio Magno · Troja
Kellits · Ewarton · Castleton · Botanical Gardens
Crofts Hill · ST. CATHERINE · Riversdale · Glengoffe · Mt. Telegraph 1275m
Linstead

comes in, it is an impressive sight – sunbathers on the beach opposite have a front-row seat. Behind the beach is a large shopping complex, which includes the Tourist Board Office, and the **Craft Market** is nearby. You can get a taste of real Jamaica in the **Vegetable Market**, which sprawls back from the main road near the clock tower. Amid the noisy crowds inside, exotic (and familiar) fruit and vegetables are piled in a rainbow of colours, from huge hanks of green bananas to scarlet peppers and orange pumpkins. The market also sells a wide variety of other items, including clothes. It is full of local atmosphere – not

A flower lady in full bloom

Colourful sports at Turtle Beach

easy to find in Ochi.
Open: every day, but much
better at the end of the week.
For a wonderful panorama of
the resort and the jungly
hillsides rising behind the
coast, it is well worth visiting
Shaw Park, set on the steep
slopes above the centre of
Ocho Rios. It has 34 acres (14
hectares) of lush, landscaped
grounds, brimming with
beautiful flowers and birds.
There are neatly-manicured
gardens as well as wilder,
wooded areas, with bubbling
streams and waterfalls.
Open: daily 09.00–17.00hrs.
The central public beach is
Turtle Beach (you pay a small
entrance fee); this semi-
circular curve of shimmering
sand, with palms scattered
along its length, turns into
Mallard's Beach around the
northeastern end of the
sheltered bay. Here there are
private stretches in front of the
two big hotels. The beach has
lots of facilities, including
watersports; there are also
plenty of bars, restaurants and
shops. Most of the sandy coves

along the coast to the east are
for the exclusive use of guests
of the hotels sitting behind
them – but there is a stretch of
public sand in the bay by the
mouth of White River (about
three miles (5km) east). And a
few miles west is **Dunn's River
Beach**, a very pretty sandy
beach surrounded by rocks
covered in dense foliage, with
Dunn's River Falls cascading
down the hill behind – it can
only be reached by paying to
go into the grounds around the
Falls.

Accommodation
Ochi has a very wide range of
accommodation from which to
choose, from exceptionally
classy hotels to cabins and
camping. There are several
hotels near the centre,
including big high-rise blocks
behind the beach, as well as
small hotels, guest houses and
rooms elsewhere around the
town – and others scattered
along the coast to the east.
Secluded amid lush tropical

gardens, on slopes and cliffs beside private coves east of the resort, are three eminently elegant (and expensive) hotels. The long-established **Jamaica Inn** (tel: 974 2514) is serenely sophisticated and beautifully appointed, with a personal atmosphere and old-world charm – in the past, it entertained guests such as Noël Coward, Claudette Colbert and Winston Churchill. The picturesque pastel pink and white **Sans Souci Hotel Club and Spa** (tel: 974 2353) is extremely stylish; it has extensive spa facilities and one of the pools is fed by Sans Souci's own mineral spring; the restaurant is excellent.

The **Plantation Inn** (tel: 974 5601) is tasteful and tranquil, with a high standard of traditional service.

Next to the Plantation Inn is **Sandals Ocho Rios** (tel: 974 5691), an all-inclusive hotel offering similar attractions to its sister hotels in Montego Bay and Negril; **Sandals Dunn's River** (tel: 972 1610) has just opened on the coast the other side of Ochi, near the waterfalls. Lying several miles east of the town, **Couples** (tel: 974 4271) is another very popular all-inclusive hotel, with lots of sports and activities for couples only. On the coast about 12 miles (19km) east, near Oracabessa, is **Boscobel Beach** (tel: 974 3330) which is also all-inclusive, but this hotel is unusual in that it is specifically aimed at families, with lots of activities for children (reminiscent of a large, fancy, tropical holiday camp).

On the coast a couple of miles east of Ochi, in an attractive bayside setting near the mouth of the White River, is the **Shaw Park Beach Hotel** (tel: 974 2552), a lively, comfortable, standard modern hotel with a popular disco. In a similar price bracket is the big, busy, rather impersonal, American-style high-rise hotel **Mallards Beach** (tel: 974 2201) on the beach close to the centre of town. The neighbouring **Divi Jamaica** (tel: 974 2151), offering all-inclusive rates, is very similar in style and facilities. Further round the beach is **Turtle Beach Towers** (tel: 974 2801), with modern self-catering apartments in high-rise blocks. All hotels mentioned above have a wide range of facilities including pools.

Between these big hotels is the simple but reasonably-priced **Inn On The Beach** (tel: 974 2782). If you do not mind not being by the beach, much the best bet for the budget-conscious is the homely and very appealing **Hibiscus Lodge** (tel: 974 2676). It is not far from the centre of town, perched on the cliffs – there are steps down to a bathing area – with pretty terraces, gardens, a pool, a good restaurant and rather Mediterranean atmosphere. The **Little Pub Inn** (tel: 974 5825) is a lively guest house in the heart of town, offering night-time entertainment.

Set on the slopes behind a

picturesque bay, about 20 miles (32km) east of Ocho Rios near Port Maria is the **Casa Maria** (tel: 994 2324). This is an attractive, small hotel at reasonable rates; the beach below is poor for bathing, but it has a pool. About five miles (8km) west of Ocho Rios, on the road by Mammee Bay, is the simple, friendly, low-priced **Arawak Inn** (tel: 972 2318), which has a pool, restaurant and disco.

Nightlife and Entertainment

As you would expect, Ochi is a centre offering many excursions. Your hotel or the local Tourist Board can give you details of the different companies and tours – there are trips all over the island, by coach or helicopter. You can also go for a 'party' cruise by sailing schooner along the coast, with lunch, snorkelling and music – or enjoy the romantic sunset and moonlight on an evening cruise. Glass-bottomed boat trips are available from beaches. (Many excursions are listed under the **What Else To See** section on page 48, and for other areas of the island.)

One of the organised trips is **An Evening on the White River**, where you are taken by fishing canoe up the torchlit river, to stop for a buffet supper, entertainment including a folklore show, and dancing under the stars – it is very similar to its Montego Bay counterpart on the Great River (see page 24). A regular **Reggae Lobster Party** is held at the Coconut Grove House,

behind the Coconut Grove shopping centre.

Otherwise you can find quite a variety of buzzing nightlife in Ochi. For example, the **Little Pub** on Main Street puts on shows celebrating island folklore with music and dance – it also has a restaurant (and late shopping). The larger hotels have evening entertainment. And popular discos include **Silks** at the Shaw Park Beach Hotel, and **Maroons** at the Divi Jamaica hotel. If you want to kick up your heels with the locals, try the **Acropolis Disco** on Main Street in the Mutual Security Mall, or for the more adventurous the **Roof Top** on James Avenue.

Restaurants

If eating out, there is lots of choice here – from glamorous restaurants (especially in the smart hotels) to take-away burgers and fried chicken. Several hotels, both great and small, have good restaurants. The **Almond Tree** (tel: 974 2676) at the Hibiscus Lodge, 21 Fort George Street, is a popular place offering a good choice of tasty dishes at reasonable prices; and the ambience is lovely, on an open-air terrace overlooking the sea, dining by candle and starlight at night.

The Ruins, DaCosta Drive, (tel: 974 2789) offers a pretty setting beside gardens with sparkling waterfalls and lily ponds, at the bottom of the hill behind the centre of the town; it is much frequented by tourists although the food is mediocre. If you decide to have more than a cocktail try one of the Chinese specialities (it also has a cheaper fast-food section). There is steel band music in the evening.

Lying on the banks of the White River, below the road bridge a couple of miles east of Ochi, is a very atmospheric Rasta restaurant called the **Jungle Lobster House** (no phone) which serves brilliant food. The rickety wooden shack sits in the shade of banana palms looking out over a cluster of fishing huts and canoes; inside on the earth floors are two long wooden tables with benches, and you can watch the fish, chicken and lobster being cooked on an open-flame stove, to the sound of reggae music. It is welcoming and good value, although the lobster is not cheap.

Harmony Hall (tel: 974 4478) is a picturesque 19th-century gingerbread house four miles (6km) east of Ochi (see page 38). Apart from the art gallery and gift shop, it has a small restaurant with an open-air patio by the garden, offering a nice selection of local, oriental and American dishes.

Shopping

Ochi is a top favourite for shopping in Jamaica, with a wealth of shops selling duty-free goods, such as cameras or perfume, and plenty of everyday shops, such as supermarkets and pharmacies. There are several plazas, including the largest on the island, **Ocean Village**, behind the centre of the beach. It has all sorts of shops: boutiques selling T-shirts and batik clothes, others with a good range of duty-free watches, jewellery, electronic equipment, fine linens, crystal and china, as well as record, book and health-food shops, and even a beauty salon; craft shops here include **The Craft Cottage**.

Just down the road, nearer Turtle Beach Towers, is **Taj Mahal**, a shopping complex

The Ruins Restaurant

also with duty-free shops; the **Treasure Chest** sells a variety of Jamaican crafts and souvenirs, while **The Collection** offers batik, tie-dyed and painted clothes (it also has branches at Ocean Village and Pineapple Place). Further east along Main Street is the **Island Plaza**, with a very good selection of shops; they include the **Frame Centre Gallery**, with fine art and wood sculptures, and **Coconut Joe** which has some great Bob Marley T-shirts.

Pineapple Place is a neat complex of pretty pink-painted shops, along the road going east out of Ochi. **Coconut Grove** lies further east, opposite the Plantation Inn.

Fishy business at Pineapple Place

Duty-free goods abound in both shopping centres. Coconut Grove also has some white chalets outside selling items such as crafts and souvenirs.

Adjacent to Ocean Village is the **Craft Market**, an enclosure full of stalls selling a bright array of handicrafts – wood-carvings, shell and coral jewellery, drums and whistles, straw hats and baskets, paintings – as well as printed T-shirts and shorts, or beaded hairbraiding. It is also worth having a quick look around the **Vegetable Market**, for stalls (for instance along the pavements outside) selling cheap souvenirs, from T-shirts to tambourines – best visited at the end of the week. Don't forget to haggle over your purchases with the 'higglers' at both markets.

Finally (but by no means least), you can find some high-quality Jamaican art, crafts, gifts and a few antique items at **Harmony Hall**, east of Ocho Rios. There are shopping excursions for visitors organised from some hotels.

Sports
There are plenty of watersports facilities from larger hotels or the main town beach – with opportunities for diving, deep-sea fishing, sailing, windsurfing, waterskiing and others. Golf and horse-riding are also available for participants, and polo for spectators, at **Chukka Cove** and **St Ann's Polo Club**. Ask at your hotel or the Tourist Board.

◆◆◆
RUNAWAY BAY

Tradition has it that this evocative name originated because it is the place where the Spanish were said to have fled to after their final defeat by the British. But it may be more likely that it gained its name from the runaway slaves who took off to Cuba from here. It is claimed that both the Spanish and the slaves sought refuge in the nearby **Runaway Caves**. Whatever the truth, it is now a popular resort area. Runaway Bay has no real town or centre – it is a relatively recent development, planned for tourists, spread along the coastal strip and main road (running into Salem at the eastern end). Along the coast are narrow stretches of sand and coral rocks. Green, wooded hills rise just south of the coast road, with views of mountains further inland.

This resort is quite simple, straightforward and unpretentious; it lacks the pockets of sophistication boasted by both Montego Bay and Ocho Rios, and the unique style of Negril. It has a reasonable range of facilities – especially at hotels – including sports. And lying so centrally on the north coast, about 17 miles (27km) west of Ocho Rios, it is convenient to reach sights and other entertainment elsewhere along the coast and on the island. Five miles (8km) west of here is **Discovery Bay**, a quiet little place which has better bathing than Runaway Bay and provides some accommodation.

Runaway Bay, where the sand and sea go on and on, thataway . . .

Accommodation

There is a variety of accommodation, but the range is more limited than in the major resorts. There are no ultra-classy, ultra-expensive hotels here – however, the area does have plenty of self-catering properties.

Among the higher-priced are some all-inclusive hotels set by stretches of sand and low cliffs, with extensive facilities. The most expensive of these is **Eaton Hall Hotel and Villas** (tel: 973 3503), which is designed in Spanish and English styles, rather smart with a personal atmosphere. **Jamaica Jamaica** (tel: 973 2436) is the largest hotel in the resort, with an imaginative range of non-stop activities, and its own golf course. The **Franklin D Resort** (tel: 973 3067) is a pastel pink complex, which includes facilities for children.

In a similar price-bracket is the lively **Club Caribbean** (tel: 973 3507), with lots of little cottages clustered behind the beach (kitchenettes are available) and a good range of facilities included free. The

CENTRAL NORTH COAST

rather more moderately-priced **Ambiance** (tel: 973 2067) is a comfortable, modern hotel, close to beach areas a little way to the east of the main strip of accommodation; it also has a wide range of facilities for visitors.

Two neat little hotels at very reasonable prices are the **Silver Spray** (tel: 973 3413), by the sea, and the **Tamarind Tree** (tel: 973 2678), on the inland side of the road.

Good value for the budget-conscious can be found at the **Caribbean Isle** (tel: 973 2364), which is a pleasant, friendly place, set by a strip of sand near the Ambiance hotel (see above).

Alternatively, try the **Runaway Bay HEART Country Club** (tel: 973 2671), where young Jamaicans train to work in the tourist business. It is quiet, and lies in pretty gardens on a hillside off the coast road – with a good restaurant. The **Salem Guest House** (no phone) is a simple, homely, little place on the inland side of the main road.

The hotels and guest house mentioned above all have pools.

If you prefer self-catering accommodation, there is a wide range. For example, **Sunflower Villas** (tel: 973 2171) offer some moderately-priced and more luxurious villas, spread behind the beach and on a quiet estate in the hills, with pools and various watersports.

Chukka Cove Villas (tel: 974 2239) have very well-appointed, up-market two-storey villas, set in peaceful, pretty gardens beside rocky coves by the Chukka Cove equestrian and polo centre, a few miles east of Runaway Bay; they have a pool.

Five miles (8km) west of Runaway Bay, at Discovery Bay, are the relaxed and friendly **Portside Villas and Apartments** (tel: 973 2007), overlooking the bay and beach; built in attractive Georgian style, they are very well-equipped and comfortably furnished, with a pool and restaurant – at very reasonable rates. For information on Sunflowers, Portside and other villas, contact the Jamaica Association of Villas and Apartments (JAVA) in the UK or US (see page 115). Croal Island Associates offer a couple of villas around Discovery Bay (tel: 965 2536 in

Jamaica, or 302-539 6198 in the US).

Nightlife and Entertainment

Runaway Bay is well located for visiting sights in the area and all over the island. Details of organised trips are available from larger hotels. Many of the Ocho Rios-based excursions are offered from Runaway Bay. You can take boat trips from hotel beaches. The larger hotels have a variety of evening entertainment. There are also discos at the **Club Caribbean**, **Ambiance** and **Tamarind Tree**. Discovery Bay is a much quieter place to stay, as there are no hotels.

Restaurants

There is a limited choice around Runaway Bay, although the hotels have restaurants. For good-value Jamaican-style meals it is worth trying the guest houses like **Salem** (see above, under Accommodation). Or visit the **Cardiff Hall** restaurant (tel: 973 2671) at **Runaway Bay HEART Country Club**. The **Recovery** (no phone) is a typical, very simple little bar and restaurant, opposite the Ambiance hotel, serving large portions of delicious local food at low prices; it is a friendly place, where you eat to the sound of reggae music and can watch locals playing dominoes in the bar.

Runaway Bay and Discovery Bay have several little bars and stalls selling snacks. For jerk pork try **El Africano**, an open, wooden rondavel bar by the roadside between the two

resorts. The Portside Villas and Apartments in Discovery Bay has a restaurant called the **Sea Shanty** (tel: 973 2007), in a lovely setting on a wooden veranda built over the sea with views of the bay.

The Mug (tel: 972 1018) is also in a pretty position on St Ann's Bay with a pleasant breezy patio right on the sea, 10 miles (16km) east of Runaway Bay; it is simple, good value and serves tasty local specialities including fish.

Shopping

Shopping facilities are quite basic in Runaway Bay and Discovery Bay although there is all you need for everyday requirements – including supermarkets and pharmacies. There are a few shopping complexes: the Northern Shopping Centre and E & W Plaza in Salem, to the east, also Columbus Plaza. However, craft stalls beside the road, for example around Salem, or just west of Discovery Bay outside Columbus Park, attract many visitors. **Discovery Bay Designs** is a shop selling Jamaican crafts and gifts. Shopping excursions to Ocho Rios are run from several hotels and self-catering complexes.

Sports

Again, larger hotels have plenty on offer – especially watersports. There is a good diving school at the Club Caribbean. Runaway Bay has a golf course just inland. Horse-riding tours and events are available at Chukka Cove Farm.

WHAT ELSE TO SEE AROUND THE CENTRAL NORTH COAST

◆
BOB MARLEY MAUSOLEUM
In a remote mountain setting south of Runaway Bay – about 25 miles (40km) by narrow, potholed roads that wind sharply round the steep slopes – is the tomb of the reggae superstar and Rasta hero, Bob Marley, who died of cancer in 1981. Although it is of limited interest to anyone who is not a fan, part of the pleasure of visiting it is the drive through beautiful, unspoilt countryside. At the bottom of the slope beneath the tomb is a café full of Rastas. They will take you up the hill to see where Marley was laid to rest – after a greeting of handshaking and 'one love'. The Lion of Judah is depicted on the stained glass windows, and inside are pictures of Marley and Haile Selassie. Every 6 February they hold an all-night concert here, to celebrate Marley's birthday.

◆◆
BRIMMER HALL PLANTATION
This plantation is in a lovely spot, with its bright white, 18th-century Great House perched on a hillside, surrounded by slopes covered in palm groves, sugar cane, green pastures and various tropical trees. This is a working plantation offering entertaining yet educational tours of its well-kept old estate, to show how the crops are cultivated and harvested – including coconuts, bananas, pineapples, coffee, sugar cane, cocoa and pimento. Visitors are taken in a tractor-drawn jitney (open wagon), and the route passes not far from the houses where Noël Coward and Ian Fleming lived. Brimmer Hall has an attractive restaurant serving Jamaican specialities, a bar, souvenir shops and swimming pool. The plantation is about six miles (9km) southwest of Port Maria, 18 miles (29km) southeast of Ocho Rios.
Open: daily 09.00 to 17.00, tours at 11.00, 13.30 and 15.30hrs (for about an hour).

◆◆
BROWN'S TOWN
This picturesque market town gives a vibrant taste of traditional rural Jamaica, just nine miles (14km) from the north coast (south of Runaway and Discovery bays). The main street is lined with shops and bars in old wooden buildings with upper verandas and open fronts. There are masses of stalls around the market area: piles of fruit and vegetables, from ackee to oranges, yams or plantains; others selling clothes, household goods, beer, popcorn; heaps of sugar cane against a fence with a boy cutting it into an oildrum; and a fried fish shack painted Rasta colours. It is full of life and noise, with donkeys carrying loads, music and rumbling lorries.
To the north, nearer the coast, are a couple of old plantation estates with Great Houses in undulating, wooded

See the light at Discovery Bay

countryside, such as Orange Valley (tours can be arranged).

◆
CIRCLE 'B' FARM

Lying uphill from the coast, this award-winning farm offers half-hour walking tours to see the wide range of crops (and livestock). These include bananas, coconuts, pineapples, water-melons and citrus fruits, as well as vegetables like okra, callaloo (spinach) and cucumbers. Visitors are offered a taste of all these. The farm offers a buffet lunch of typical Jamaican dishes, and it has a bar and picnic area. Almost halfway between Runaway Bay and Ocho Rios, about three miles (5km) south of the main coast road.
Open: daily 10.00–17.00hrs.

◆
DISCOVERY BAY

A splendid, sheltered bay – traditionally Columbus landed here – with palm-wooded hills rising behind and curving around to the western headland. It is dominated by a big bauxite plant and terminal, covered in red dust – according to visitors, after a while it seems less intrusive and it can even be quite interesting watching the ships negotiating the coral reefs as they enter the bay. Set high above the sea, on the cliff-tops to the west, is **Columbus Park**, an open-air museum with panoramic views over the bay. The bay has a small, quiet resort and modern settlement towards its eastern side. This side of Discovery Bay is called Puerto Seco (Dry Harbour – as named by Columbus) where there is a public beach, a rather narrow stretch of pale sand offering better bathing than Runaway Bay as it is less shallow and rocky underwater. There is a water play-area for children, and green park land behind it – a popular spot for picnics. Nearby is a small shopping complex, including a supermarket and bike hire; there are also bars and a restaurant. It lies five miles (8km) west of Runaway Bay.

Against the tide: Dunn's River Falls

◆◆◆
DUNN'S RIVER FALLS
Jamaica has many lovely
waterfalls, but these are the
most famous – a major
attraction. However, despite its
popularity the site avoids
feeling too commercial. Cool
mountain waters cascade
dramatically over smooth
limestone rocks and terraces,
into bubbling pools; altogether
tumbling 600 feet (183m) to
where it streams under the
main road onto a beautiful
beach below. A favourite sport
is to climb the falls: starting
from the beach, visitors can
climb in a group, all holding
hands in a chain, led by a
guide who carries everyone's
cameras around his neck and
shouts encouragement. It takes
about half an hour and is great
fun. The short climb is mostly
quite gentle, although it is

steep in a few places, and you
have to watch for slippery
rocks or strong torrents of
water – you can make your
exit early if it becomes too
tiring. Otherwise you can
watch these amusing antics
from wooden platforms beside
the falls. Climbers will get very
wet, so swimwear is essential
(and shoes like trainers might
be useful) – there are
changing rooms and lockers
for your clothes and valuables
on the beach. Dunn's River
Falls lies about two miles (3km)
west of Ocho Rios.
Open: daily 08.00–17.00hrs.

◆
FERN GULLY
Climbing up the steep hills
south of Ocho Rios, the main
road snakes along the path of
an old river bed. The three-
mile (5km) stretch known as
Fern Gully is bordered by
sheer, rocky sides, and
carpeted by hundreds of
species of ferns. Some of the
trees were damaged by
Hurricane Gilbert in 1988, but
not enough to detract from its
character – and foliage grows
very quickly here.

◆◆◆
FIREFLY
On a plateau, about 1,000 feet
(300m) above the coast, is the
surprisingly modest little house
that Noël Coward had built in
1956. The witty playwright and
composer spent much time
here and the absolutely
stupendous views inspired his
song, *A Room With A View*.
You can see right along the
coastline, with bays and

headlands where the forested hills plunge down to the sea. No wonder Coward fell in love with this place. Inside it is much as he left it when he died, and is maintained by the National Trust as a museum, with his two baby grand pianos, writing desk, and various memorabilia like manuscripts, paintings, records, even his clothes. Coward's grave lies behind the house, protected by a large white cage. The house is reached some distance up a steep, winding dirt road, off the main coast road about four miles (6km) east of Oracabessa, 17 miles (27km) east of Ocho Rios. *Open*: Monday to Saturday, 09.00–16.00hrs. A little below Firefly is the stone ruin of a building. Legend has it that this is Henry Morgan's 'pirate lair', with musket-firing slits and an escape tunnel. This spot was called Look-Out, before Coward christened it after the fireflies that twinkled all around when he first visited it. Further down the road, near the sea, is Goldeneye, the house Ian Fleming owned for nearly 20 years and where he invented James Bond. It is closed to the public.

◆◆
HARMONY HALL
This very pretty 'gingerbread' house is a restored Victorian manse dating from 1886, which was part of a pimento estate. Built of stone and white-painted woodwork, with a green shingled roof and pointed tower, it has exquisite lacy wooden fretwork around the eaves and upper veranda, referred to as gingerbread fretwork. Outside steps lead up to the veranda where there is an art gallery and craft shop on the first floor. There are displays of some wonderful work by contemporary Jamaican artists, as well as high-quality crafts and gifts; it also has special exhibitions. It is worth coming to have a look – as well as trying the pleasant restaurant on the ground floor and garden patio. By the main coast road about four miles (6km) east of Ocho Rios. *Open*: daily, gallery 10.00–18.00hrs, restaurant and bar 11.00–24.00hrs.

The view from Firefly

CENTRAL NORTH COAST

◆
ORACABESSA

This little, local port gained its name from the Spanish (*ora* and *cabeza*, meaning Golden Head), and it sits on a green, wooded hillside, to one side of a creek. It is a typical sleepy village of wooden buildings – some with lacy fretwork around the verandas, many rather rickety – with a market place near the centre. Just to the northeast is a track leading to the sea (opposite an Esso petrol station), where there is a pocket-handkerchief-sized sandy beach which is very sheltered. There are usually traditional fishing canoes and fishing cages on the beach. It also has a simple refreshment shack. Oracabessa lies 13 miles (21km) east of Ocho Rios, and driving eastwards from here, you will see some of Jamaica's loveliest coastal landscapes.

◆
PORT MARIA

This bustling town is set above a huge, rocky bay, and there are views of the coastline with its splendid headlands and verdant hills. Once a busy banana port, it is now a market and fishing town. In the shopping centre, the streets are lined with stalls, fruit and vegetables are piled high on the pavement, and there are lots of shops and bar shacks; a big market is held here on Friday and Saturday. A bridge joins this part to a quieter residential area. The town has a courthouse and an Anglican church (on the outskirts) dating from the 19th century. A sign directs you to the Tacky Monument, dedicated to the leader of the 1760 slave rebellion.

On the edge of Port Maria are the ruins of a fort. An open, palm-thatched jerk chicken bar by the sea offers lovely views of the bay. The main road continues south out of town, going inland through lush forested hills, banana plantations and coconut groves. Port Maria lies 21 miles (34km) east of Ocho Rios.

◆◆◆
PROSPECT PLANTATION

This is one of the most popular plantation tours. It combines a glimpse of spectacular scenery, including forested hills, mountains and valleys, as well as interesting information on the crops and plants of Jamaica, and some of the island's history. Visitors are taken round the huge estate of around 1,000 acres (400 hectares) in a tractor-drawn jitney (open wagon), and are shown crops like pineapples, sugar cane, bananas, coffee, cassava, pimento (allspice), coconuts, cocoa, pawpaw and other fruit. The guides are very knowledgeable, and make the trip very entertaining – climbing a tree to pick a coconut, giving you samples to taste or spicy leaves to smell. You will also learn about some of the exotic trees and pretty flowers; lots of the trees here have been planted by famous visitors, and bear plaques with names like Noël Coward, Winston Churchill, Prince

Prospect Plantation – glorious scenery and fascinating history

Philip, Charlie Chaplin, Henry Kissinger and Ian Fleming. It is a peaceful (if rather bumpy) ride and worth it for the dramatic views, such as of the White River Gorge, where the river rushes over rocks far below the sheer forested hillsides. And from Sir Harold's Viewpoint there are splendid panoramas of the hills, coastline, and the early 18th-century Great House, where the owner Lady Mitchell (Sir Harold's widow) lives.

Apart from the jitney tour (which takes about an hour), you can take horse rides around the plantation (book an hour in advance). The estate also has an 18-hole mini-golf course, and a rondavel bar at the entrance. Prospect lies just off the main road, about four miles (6km) east of Ocho Rios. *Open*: daily, tours Monday to Saturday 10.30, 14.00 and 15.30hrs, Sunday 11.00, 13.30 and 15.00hrs.

◆
RIO BUENO

Once a busy port, now a quaint fishing village, the horseshoe-shaped bay also has claims on being the site where Columbus first landed. There are several architectural reminders of past colonial days. **New Gallery Jo James** has paintings and woodcarvings, as well as a small restaurant. There is also a roadside stop with souvenir and craft stalls. Rio Bueno lies six miles (9km) west of Discovery Bay.

◆
RUNAWAY CAVES AND GREEN GROTTO

These limestone caves, whose passageways stretch for miles, are said to have given refuge to the Spanish, runaway slaves and pirates. The caverns feature a variety of extraordinary stalactite and stalagmite formations – some are hollow and the guide plays primitive 'tunes' on them with a stick. You will also see bats hiding in the nooks and crannies. The Green Grotto – so-called because of the green algae on the rocks – lies 120 feet (36m) underground. It is an eerie, vaulted chamber containing a lake, on which you can take a boat trip; this underground tidal lake is a mixture of fresh and salt water, and is inhabited by fish (including crayfish and mullet) which are blind. Inside the entrance of the caves is a small bar and souvenir stalls, with a reggae guitarist playing music that echoes around the cavern. The tour covers about a mile (1.6km), and takes around 45 mins.

These caves are usually the most popular with visitors, as they are more accessible than others on the island, lying a little more than two miles (3km) west of Runaway Bay. Outside the caves is a 160 foot (49m)-deep lagoon.

Open: daily 09.00–17.00hrs.

◆
ST ANN'S BAY

This town is set on the slopes rising inland off the main road, which runs beside the big sheltered bay – further out you can see a line of white waves in the turquoise sea, where they break on the coral reef. The palm-covered hills behind the bay ascend to mountains further inland. Along the narrow streets in town, are typical old clapboard buildings with overhanging upper verandas forming arcades over the pavements. It has a busy shopping centre, with all sorts of shops, little restaurants and bars. A market, with stalls and piles of produce, lines a steep central street. It was here that Marcus Garvey was born, and his statue stands in front of the library. The town also has a 19th-century courthouse and 18th-century fort. Beside the bay is a simple little restaurant, **The Mug**, with a pleasant, breezy patio, which serves

Scuba diving at St Ann's Bay

delicious fresh fish at very reasonable prices. St Ann's Bay is seven miles (11km) west of Ocho Rios and 10 miles (16km) east of Runaway Bay. Just west of St Ann's Bay is the site of **Seville Neuva**, the Spanish colonist's first capital (which was abandoned in 1534), near the statue of Columbus and Seville Great House. The scant ruins are being excavated and reconstructed, with plans to open an archaeological park on the Seville estate.

A little further east is Drax Hall, where there is a pretty, palm-fringed, sandy beach called **Mammee Bay**, with smart villas set in gardens behind it. On the coast nearby is the St Ann's Polo Club.

◆

WHITE RIVER RAFTING

This is an enjoyable way to see some of the scenery along the lower reaches of the White River including the hills rising steeply either side, covered in green, jungle foliage which forms canopies over the waterway. It is conveniently close to Ocho Rios (you take the raft from the White River Reggae Park, a small area near the bridge where the main road crosses the river, about two miles (3km) east of the resort) – however, if you have time, it is worth trying one of the other rafting trips which are better. This one takes you up and downstream to the sea, in a long bamboo raft, and covers about a mile (1.6km) in 45 minutes.
Open: daily 09.00–17.00hrs.

THE NORTHEAST

This small area, mostly lying in the parish of Portland – the northern part of the county of Surrey – boasts some of the best Jamaica has to offer. It is much less touristy than other parts of the north coast, and has only one resort, Port Antonio.

Here there is some of the island's most stunning scenery, both along the coast and inland. The rugged coast sweeps up to voluptuous hills, rising to the high inland peaks of the Blue Mountains, which are usually bathed in misty clouds. The northeast tradewinds, meeting the high land, sprinkle more rain in this area than elsewhere on the island. Consequently the tropical foliage is at its most vibrant and luscious.

All around the northeast visitors encounter endless breathtaking views of the coastline and mountains inland. The northern part of this coast is indented with bays – where there are often sleepy little fishing villages, their canoes drawn up on the beach – and high, wooded headlands, which plunge directly down to the sea, with cliffs in many places. There are banana plantations and coconut groves along the coast, as well as pastures with cattle grazing.

The landscapes are especially striking just east of Port Antonio, where picturesque coves pepper the coast, backed by steep slopes shrouded in the most profuse

THE NORTHEAST

and verdant vegetation. This part has some of the island's loveliest, most secluded beaches. Although the coast west of here has beaches of grey shingly sand and rocks, around Port Antonio and the east coast the sand becomes pale and silvery again. If you enjoy beaches where the waves come rolling in, you'll find them here. The east is more windswept, with surf-splashed rocky cliffs and deserted stretches of sand backed by coconut palms and patches of dense jungle.

The main road, which winds all around the coast, is much quieter here – and very potholed due to the heavy rains (and Hurricane Gilbert). The northeast is mostly quite unspoilt by tourism; although Port Antonio has accommodation for visitors, including some plush hotels and villas scattered along the coast to the east, it is very low-key compared to other northern resorts.

This is an area to visit if you want peace and quiet,

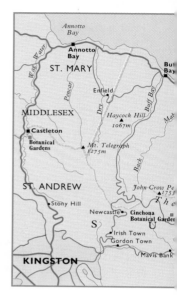

although Port Antonio has a sophisticated side to it that is missing on the south coast (with the exception of Kingston).

Taking the banana trail – bamboo rafts which once carried fruit are now a tourist's treat

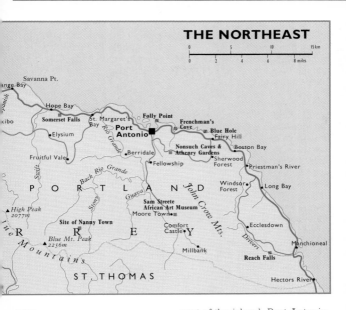

THE NORTHEAST

◆◆◆
PORT ANTONIO

This could well claim to be Jamaica's most enchanting coastal resort town. In the early days, the rugged terrain and thick jungle deterred extensive settlement in this

part of the island. Port Antonio started expanding in the late 19th century, when the banana trade began. By the 1920s and 1930s, this had become the world's banana capital. It started declining shortly afterwards, partly because of the devastating effects on the crops of Panama Disease and the hurricanes. Bananas were carried down the Rio Grande on bamboo rafts – which are now used to transport tourists instead. And in Port Antonio's heyday, locals carried huge bunches of bananas on their heads, singing to help them bear the heavy loads and hard work – just like the 'Banana Boat Song' made famous by Harry Belafonte.

Port Antonio was a popular spot with visitors long before

Montego Bay or Ocho Rios. The development of tourism at the beginning of the century was closely linked with the banana trade: an enterprising entrepreneur started bringing North American passengers to Port Antonio on the empty banana boats that were coming to collect their cargo. Later, it thrived as a romantic hideaway for movie stars and other fashionable luminaries, such as Errol Flynn, Bette Davis, Clara Bow, Ginger Rogers, William Randolph Hearst and Rudyard Kipling. Flynn sailed here on his yacht in the 1940s, fell in love with Port Antonio (as many do) and bought Navy Island; his reputation for hellraising and wild parties has entered the annals of local legend. His widow still lives here, on a large ranch to the east, and runs a gift shop at the Jamaica Palace Hotel. Port Antonio still has an air of sophisticated exclusivity remaining from the days when it entertained a glittering élite. But you do not have to be either rich or famous to share its treasures. Port Antonio combines unspoilt local character with a good range of amenities for visitors in a very appealing manner. An important part of this special charm is due to its beautiful setting. It sits beside superb twin harbours, flanked by Navy Island, nestling in the close embrace of luxuriantly wooded hillsides, with a backdrop of soaring, blue-tinged mountain peaks. Rivers flow into both **West** and **East Harbour**, and the busy centre

lies behind the harbours. Jutting out between these two deep, sheltered bays is a peninsula bluff on which is a quieter residential district – once the most exclusive part of town, there are some fine examples of Victorian gingerbread architecture here.

Around the town can be seen typical, clapboard houses, their balustraded upper verandas (some decorated with gingerbread fretwork) shading the streets below. At the junction of Harbour Street and West Street is a square with a clock tower and an old red-brick **courthouse**, its white stone-work, columns and wrought-iron veranda sparkling in the sun. Just up Harbour Street, in the City Centre Plaza, is the local Tourist Board office; further along is **Christ Church**, an imposing stone Anglican parish church, dating from 1840.

West Street is the main thoroughfare lying behind West Harbour. In a big building, opposite a little square with a cenotaph monument, is the **Town Market** which sells piles of colourful fruit (including different varieties of banana) and vegetables, as well as some crafts and gifts; the best market days are towards the end of the week. Also on West Street is the entrance to the **Huntress Marina**, where there are plush yachts and deep-sea fishing boats moored beside the jetty – on which is a palm-thatched bar, ideal for sitting to

Port Antonio Harbour

watch the activity in the harbour. Port Antonio is renowned for its deep-sea fishing, especially blue marlin. Nearby, you can take the quaint little passenger ferry (every half hour, from 07.00 to 01.00hrs) to **Navy Island** – which was sold by Mrs Errol Flynn after her husband died, but is still privately owned. Nothing remains of the large naval station that the British built here long ago. It is a pretty little wooded island, where there are three small sandy beaches; and the attractive Admiralty Club hotel (which used to be Flynn's private residence) has a restaurant, beach bars and a marina offering watersports. Little fishing canoes are pulled up on the shore, beside the main road curving around East Harbour. The north side of the harbour is protected by another peninsula, on which is the **Folly Estate**. A track leads to the ruins of a stone and concrete mansion, with grand Doric columns and dubious

graffiti. The views across the harbour to Port Antonio, with the Blue Mountains behind, provide more to look at than the building. It was built in 1905 by a rich American, for his wife who was one of the Tiffanys of New York. Local legend has it that he stocked the gardens with flowers, birds and animals – all white – but when he carried his bride over the threshold, the mansion started collapsing and his wife fled. The truth is much more prosaic: they both lived here periodically in the latter years of their life, until his death in 1912, and it was in the 1930s that the roof collapsed as the salty air corroded the reinforcement rods. Nearby, standing on the end of the peninsula, is the 100-year-old Folly Point Lighthouse. The main road continues east, hugging the coast where waves crash against the rugged coral and volcanic rocks in plumes of spray. On a headland next to one of Jamaica's loveliest hotels, the Trident, is a massive, white, Christmas-cake-style 'castle'. Locals called it Folly II, as it lay unfinished for several years in the early 1980s, when the baroness who had it built ran into problems (she also built the Jamaica Palace hotel, near by). It was rescued by the architect who designed the Trident, and this extraordinary mansion is used as his country abode.

Further east, a little road leads down to **Frenchman's Cove**. The hotel is still being repaired after being damaged by Hurricane Gilbert, but you can pay a small charge to use the enchanting beach. This little cove of soft, silver sand is sheltered by jungle-covered cliffs, and a clear, green stream meanders around the edge into the sea. The beach shelves quite steeply underwater, so the undertow can be strong; but in places the stream is deep enough to bathe in, as it runs over the sand.

A little further east is **San San Beach**, which is a public beach (there is a small admission charge). In the bay of streaked turquoise sea lies a minute islet crowned in a profuse clump of trees – Monkey Island. The beach has a variety of facilities, including a restaurant, bar, watersports and lifeguard.

The next beach is **Dragon Bay**, a small, sandy cove in similar scenic surroundings. The beach has a bar and sports facilities.

Along this winding coastal road, you will pass occasional snack stands selling jerk pork or patties, bar shacks, a craft centre and a riding stables. There are also a couple of sleepy villages hidden amongst the lush greenery. Sitting on the steps of one of the open-fronted bar-shops, visitors are treated to a colourful soap-opera of local life unfolding in the main street. The prettily named Fairy Hill is one such village; and down a precipitous rough track is **Fairy Hill Beach** (or Winefride's Beach). It is a delightful, secluded spot – little known except to locals, and a few who travel from Kingston at weekends to visit it. The weathered skeleton of a tree lies on the sand, and children play in its branches. The tranquillity is broken only by the soothing sound of waves breaking on the reef in the bay – except when locals hold a party here on Saturday night.

Accommodation

Port Antonio does not have so many hotels from which to choose, but there is a good variety of accommodation. You can find exceptional elegance at some of the properties along the coast to the east, as well as simple hotels and guest houses in town or along the road going east.

The **Trident Villas and Hotel** (tel: 993 2602) is outstandingly classy (with high prices to match); it occupies a fine postion on a rocky headland just east of town, next to a tiny private sandy cove. Tastefully designed throughout, it has beautifully stylish, spacious villas set right by the crashing waves in immaculate gardens, with a pool and strutting peacocks; there is also an elegant restaurant. It is quite small, and has a serene, secluded and personal atmosphere.

Close by, sitting in imposing splendour on the inland side of the road overlooking a rocky bay, is the more moderately priced **Jamaica Palace Hotel** (tel: 993 2021). This grand, sparkling-white edifice mixes neo-classical style with a Middle Eastern flavour; there is a Jamaica-shaped pool in the gardens.

The **Admiralty Club** (tel: 993 2267) on Navy Island is very different. Formerly Errol Flynn's residence, it is now a hotel complex with cottages and huts sprinkled over the island – kitchenettes or hot-plates are available for self-caterers, although it has a good restaurant. Rates are moderate and there is a variety of facilities. The **Marbella Club** (tel: 993 3281) has villas lying in pretty gardens by Dragon Bay beach, about six miles (9km) east of Port Antonio. It has a pool and various sports facilities.

High on a very steep hillside behind San San Bay, just west of here, is the **Fern Hill Club** (tel: 993 3222), set in 40 acres (16 hectares) of tropical foliage. This reasonably priced all-inclusive hotel offers very good value.

Lying 600 feet (183m) above Port Antonio, with stupendous panoramas of its harbours and the mountains to the south, is the **Bonnie View Plantation Hotel** (tel: 993 2752). It nestles in 25 acres (10 hectares) of grounds on a hilltop, and is one of the oldest hotels in the Caribbean. Modest but homely, relaxed and peaceful – facilities include a pool and horse-riding – it is ideal for the budget-conscious.

Old-fashioned, simple accommodation at reasonable prices with good food can be found at the family-run **DeMontevin Lodge** (tel: 993 2604), in a quaint

The pool at Jamaica Place Hotel

THE NORTHEAST

Victorian gingerbread house, built of red-brick with a lacy white wrought-iron balcony. There are some attractive villas on the tropical hillsides around San San Bay, offering magnificent views and seclusion – in the higher price brackets. **Goblin Hill Villas** (tel: 993 3286) are white stucco villas scattered over a lush green estate, with a pool. **San San Villas** (tel: booking: 974 2508) offer a variety of individual villas in the area, including some very luxurious properties with pools.

Nightlife and Entertainment
The **Navy Island Beach Buffet** is a lively evening of folk-dancing and fire-eating, along with an open-air dinner. The **Fern Hill Club** puts on nightly entertainment such as folk shows, beach parties or live reggae (with dinner, for which you pay an all-inclusive price). There are a few nightclubs in town, but if you want to get-on-down with the locals, go to the the funky **Roof Club** on West Street, where the reggae is throbbingly loud.

Restaurants
Several of the hotels mentioned above have restaurants worth trying. Home-style local dishes at budget-prices are offered by the **Bonnie View Hotel** (tel: 993 2752), with its splendid views, and the **DeMontevin Lodge** (tel: 993 2604), whose owner used to cook for Errol Flynn. The **Admiralty Club** (tel: 993 2267) has a popular restaurant in an attractive setting on Navy Island. For the ultimate in sophisticated dining, visit the *soigné* restaurant at the **Trident Hotel** (tel: 993 2602). (Make advance reservations for the latter three restaurants.) In town there is a variety of small restaurants serving Jamaican fare. Among these is **Daddy Dee** (no telephone) on West Street, a friendly, local bar where you can eat well and cheaply.
For a romantic ambience, try the restaurant right by the Blue Lagoon (tel: 993 2495). And for jerk pork or chicken, go to Boston Bay.

Shopping
This is not Port Antonio's long suit, although there are plenty of shops to fulfil everyday needs. The **City Centre Plaza**, on Harbour Street, has a shop selling duty-free items such as crystal, china and jewellery. The **Oasis**, in Harbour Street, has Jamaican wood and wickerwork, T-shirts, jams and books. The **Crafts Market** is at the back of the busy town market on West Street – best visited on Friday or Saturday – where you can buy wood carvings, straw baskets, sandals, T-shirts as well as exotic fruit and spices.
The **Designer's Gallery**, at the Jamaica Palace Hotel, is a boutique owned by Patrice Wymore Flynn (Errol's widow) where there is a selection of chic and fun clothing.
Next to the Jamaica Palace Hotel is a woodwork and craft centre; and at Fairy Hill, further east, is a roadside shack selling a variety of wicker items.

Sports

Some of the hotels offer facilities, such as for watersports or tennis. Watersports are also available from San San Beach or the Huntress Marina. Deep-sea fishing is excellent in the waters off Port Antonio; an international Spring Fishing Tournament (in March) and International Marlin Tournament (in October) are held here.

Two views of Blue Hole's deep and translucent waters

WHAT ELSE TO SEE IN THE NORTHEAST

◆
ANNOTTO BAY

The name of this town comes from an orange dye made from a tropical tree that used to grow here. It is a pleasant place, set on a wide bay, where two estuaries flow into the sea. The normal sleepy pace of local life here becomes colourfully lively on Saturdays, market day, when all sorts of exotic fruit and vegetables grown in this fecund area are on sale. Annotto Bay lies 29 miles (47km) west of Port Antonio.

◆◆
BLUE HOLE

Also known as the Blue Lagoon, for reasons that become clear as its waters when you see it. The lagoon, of translucent, emerald-turquoise water, is set on the rocky coast to one side of San San Bay with its lovely beach – six miles (9km) east of Port Antonio. Luxuriant, dark-green jungle cloaks the sheer slopes rising all around, shading the lagoon which is reputed to be bottomless, although the less romantic estimate around 200 feet (60m). You can swim in the waters, feeling the warm sea mixing with the cold currents from the springwater that feeds it. The romantic also say it has a rejuvenating effect, but then, if you bathed in all the waters in Jamaica that are supposed to have that effect, you would be back in your second childhood before long. From the lagoon, visitors can take a glass-bottomed boat trip (or raft) round to San San Beach and Monkey Island, a pretty little blob of jungle lying in the bay.

◆◆◆
BOSTON BAY

Connoisseurs claim this is *the* place to try Jamaica's jerk pork, and it is because of this reputation that jerk pork is often prefixed with 'Boston' at snack stands all over the island. It is sold by the pound, and can be very fatty, so specify what you want (if unsure, ask to try before you buy). This is a busy, popular spot with locals around lunchtime. And you can also buy jerk chicken, spicy sausage, festival (a crispy, deep-fried dumpling), and cold drinks to quench the fire of the piquant pork. It may not be to everyone's taste, but the beautiful beach certainly is. The brilliant aquamarine sea is good for swimming – or surfing, on the sizeable waves that roll into the bay. Boston Bay is nine miles (14km) east of Port Antonio.

◆◆
CASTLETON GARDENS

Not only are these botanical gardens a rich showcase of tropical flora, but the drive there is magnificent – as it lies almost halfway to Kingston along the 'Junction' road, in the mountainous interior. The road follows the ravine of the Wag Water River, winding precipitously round hairpin bends (watch out for buses coming thundering round the corners). Streams and waterfalls tumble down the sheer rocky sides, the slopes soar up to the Blue Mountains in the east, and the landscape is covered in a high, tangled canopy of rain forest. Castleton Gardens were founded 130 years ago, covering 15 acres (6 hectares) of what was once a sugar plantation. There are over 1,000 different species of native and exotic plants in the gardens, including many imported from South America – with 47 varieties of palm, many pretty shrubs and flowers. It is worth hiring the services of guide Roy Bennett (who learnt about the gardens from his father, who was a guide before him). He knows all the plants like the back of his hand – on which he will demonstrate the properties of the tattoo fern, that leaves a white imprint of its feathery leaves. He will also show you trees used for their wood, flowering trees like the blue mahoe (giant hibiscus, which is Jamaica's national tree) and flame of the forest, plants that produce camphor, eucalyptus, tapioca, cocoa, nutmeg, allspice, even strychnine; and he will also point out beautiful birds, as he knows where all their favourite spots are. You can bathe in the crystal-clear water, or picnic on the shady banks, watching butterflies flutter about the gardens. There is a small bar. It lies southwest of Port Antonio, 41 miles (66km) by road 12 miles (19km) south of Annotto Bay, and about 18 miles (29km) north of the centre of Kingston. *Open*: daily 06.00–18.00hrs.

◆ MOORE TOWN

This little village is the capital of the Windward Maroons. It is a difficult drive, along a steep, winding road 10 miles (16km) south of Port Antonio into the John Crow Mountains – but worth it to see the splendid, untamed landscapes. In Moore Town is Bump Grave (near the school), with a monument to show this is where the Right Excellent Nanny (warrior Queen of the Maroons) is buried.

◆◆ NONSUCH CAVES AND ATHENRY GARDENS

Set high in the hills above the coast, about three miles (5km) southeast of Port Antonio, past lush thickets of jungle, slopes carpeted with ferns and dappled with dark-green trees, the caves lie in 185 acres (75 hectares) of working copra (coconut) plantation. You wander through pretty, well-kept gardens, with labelled plants, to the entrance of the caves (discovered in 1955 by a goat). They are reckoned to be over a million years old, and were thrust up from the bed of the sea. The blow holes in the roof of the caverns were caused by swirling water – bats cluster in them now – and you can see fossilised coral and stalagmite formations, including the 'pipe organ' that plays different notes when hit. The biggest cavern, called the 'cathedral room' is 40 feet (12m) high. Outside there is a viewing platform.
Open: daily 09.00 to 17.00hrs (the tour takes 1½ hrs).

Unspoilt beauty at Reach Falls

◆◆ REACH FALLS

After the tiny fishing village of Manchioneal, on the east coast, and just before the Drivers River bridge, a rough, winding track leads towards the mountains inland along a deep, forested valley. Although there is a small wooden booth where a couple of guides sit (and you are expected to give a tip afterwards), these remote waterfalls are completely unspoilt and secluded. You walk down some narrow steps carved into the cliff beside the falls, into the gorge where water cascades over rocks into a pool overhung by foliage – you can take a dip, and find the cave behind the falls. Reach Falls are about two miles (3km) from Manchioneal, which is 21 miles (33km) southeast of Port Antonio.
Open: Saturday to Wednesday, 12.30 to 17.30 hrs.

THE NORTHEAST

◆◆◆
RIO GRANDE RAFTING

It was Errol Flynn who is said to have started organising races between the bamboo rafts that were used to transport bananas downriver. This is the longest of the rafting trips: for two and a half hours you can sit back and soak up some spectacular scenery (and a rum punch or beer), while the captain stands at the front of the raft skilfully navigating you down six miles (9km) of river. It starts high in the hills behind Port Antonio, and ends at the coast.

In places the river has sheer rocky sides, with curtains of greenery – you pass through a mossy stone archway called Lovers Lane, where you make a wish – elsewhere, it is bordered by patches of sand or pebble beach. There are stopping points with craft, drink or snack stalls, where you may also take an invigorating swim in the river. The trip ends at Rafter's Rest, on the coast, where there is a pleasant bar, restaurant and souvenir shops. There are changing facilities at both ends of the trip, but if you are wearing swimwear do take clothes to protect yourself from the hot sun. Official drivers will take your car down to Rafter's Rest (for an extra charge). They offer moonlight raft trips by arrangement. The starting point at Berridale is about six miles (9km) south of Port Antonio. Trips daily, starting 08.30 to 16.30hrs.

◆◆◆
SAM STREET'S AFRICAN ART MUSEUM

In the hills inland of Long Bay, on the east coast, in a house that used to be part of a rum factory, Dr Sam Street has a varied and personal collection of African art. It is definitely worth seeing. It lies about 15 miles (24km) southeast of Port Antonio. Take pot luck with opening hours.

◆◆
SOMERSET FALLS

This picturesque series of gentle waterfalls is set on a sheer, rocky hillside near the coast, which is cloaked in steamy jungle. You can take a gondola trip along the river to see hidden falls and caves, swim or picnic in peaceful surroundings. It lies about two miles (3km) west of Port Antonio.

Open: daily 10.00–17.00hrs.

Somerset Falls

THE SOUTHEAST

Kingston, the heart of Jamaica

This area covers the parishes of St Thomas, St Andrew and St Catherine which are in the southern part of the counties of Surrey and Middlesex. Kingston, Jamaica's capital city is located here, as well as the old capital of Spanish Town. The scenery here is quite different to the north – especially on the dry, dusty coastal plains. This is savannah landscape: golden grass wafting in the breeze, scattered with gnarled trees, spiky cacti and a few palms; the plains rise to rocky hillsides covered in bush and scrub vegetation. It only starts to look vividly green high in the hills, and around river valleys or patches of swamp on the coast.

In the rainy season, raging torrents tumble down the Blue Mountain valleys to the coast east of Kingston; during the dry season they are just mere trickles in wide, stony river beds. Just a few miles inland of the parched coastal strip, the cool slopes of the Blue Mountains are clad in green foliage, pines and coffee plantations. The soaring peaks provide a spectacular backdrop to Kingston and the coast.

The main road east of Kingston hugs the coastline, and little villages are scattered all along it. To the west, the road goes inland. Apart from the backbone of central highlands inland, there are outcrops of scrubby hills by the coast on two promontories, such as the bulge of the Hellshire Hills southwest of Kingston. From here going westwards, the coast can only be reached by road in a few places – and these roads are often narrow and rough. This part of the coast is generally sparsely inhabited; there are more little villages and towns inland, especially along the rivers. There are extensive sugar cane plantations on the plains around the southeast tip of the island and west of Kingston.

THE SOUTHEAST

There are also some coconut and banana groves by the coast in the east, and towards the west are many citrus groves (which are mainly to be found inland) and a few tobacco fields.

This is not the area to visit if a choice of good beaches is required. Although there are some stretches of pale sand lining the straight coast to the east, they are not as inviting as the bays and coves along the north. The beaches further west are more inaccessible, and some are of darker sand. The main attraction of this area is Kingston, with its wealth of Jamaican culture. And there is plenty of historic interest in Port Royal – once the colourful capital of the buccanneers – and Spanish Town.

WHAT TO SEE

◆◆
KINGSTON

Kingston is where the real, pulsating heart of Jamaica beats. The culture and commerce of the island are centred here as well as many of its people. What the city lacks in aesthetic appeal, its splendid setting more than makes up for. It sits beside a very impressive harbour – the world's seventh largest natural harbour. The Palisadoes peninsula is a long thin spit of land that curves around it to the south, where the Norman Manley Airport lies and at the western tip, Port Royal. From here you can appreciate magnificent views of the mountains rising behind

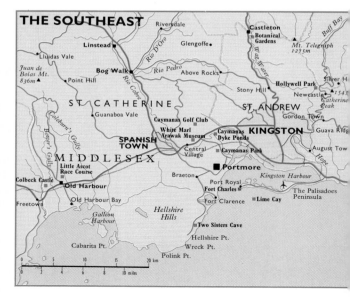

the city. Apart from the cultural and historic interest to be found in Kingston and its surroundings, you can also quickly leave the noise and dust behind by driving up into the Blue Mountains, a haven of beauty and tranquillity.

Kingston was founded in the 17th century; and after Port Royal was devastated by an earthquake in 1692, survivors flocked to Kingston. In 1872 it became the new capital of Jamaica, and the seat of government was transferred from Spanish Town. In 1907, an earthquake and fire destroyed many of the old downtown buildings. During the last 30 years, there have been major attempts at reconstruction and revitalisation. But as the population continues to swell

the city exuberantly defies these efforts to discipline and order it.

Kingston is a chaotic, crowded, melting-pot of a city, and a mishmash of different architectural styles, from appealing old colonial buildings to modern high-rise concrete blocks, and, in sharp contrast, the graffiti-daubed, scruffy tin and wood shacks of the ghetto areas in the west. The up-market residential suburbs tend to lie in the foothills, such as Beverly Hills to the east.

Numerous bars, shops and a surprising number of churches line the busy, dusty central streets; reggae throbs from many corners; there are stalls and 'higglers' selling their wares from the pavement. And

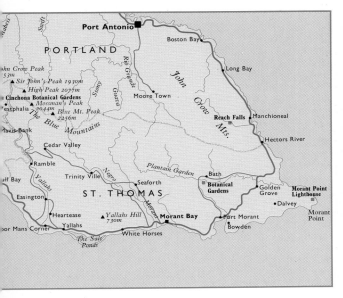

THE SOUTHEAST

in places there are even goats or pigs snuffling around. Although Kingston is less dangerous than, say, New York or Miami, it is wise to avoid certain areas like Trench Town (which has nothing of interest for the visitor, anyway). There is crime – found in any big city – but Kingston also has vitality, excitement, sophistication and all sorts of entertainment.

The **downtown** area of Kingston, or city centre, actually lies around the waterfront in the south. This was the heart of the old city, and recently the waterfront has had a facelift. The broad boulevards boast many sparkling modern buildings including a conference centre, hotels, banks, offices and shops. Quite close to the waterfront is a railway station, from where you can take a train across the island to Montego Bay. And from Pier 1 on the harbour, little water taxis leave for Port Royal. One of the attractions of the waterfront is the **Crafts Market**, in a big building in front of the piers, where you will find an excellent collection of local handicrafts. A few blocks east on Orange Street is the National Gallery. On the waterfront nearby, the big, modern Bank of Jamaica has a **Coin and Note Museum**. Further north, Orange Street is lined with colourful street stalls. Opposite Gordon House, where Jamaica's Parliament meets – and near the island's only synagogue – is **Headquarters House**. This fine

18th-century building, with white columns, was once the seat of government and the military.

Near by is **The Parade**, a spacious green square surrounded by wide boulevards, which was once the centre of Kingston. On one side is **Kingston Parish Church**, reconstructed in 1909 on original 17th-century foundations. The English Admiral John Benbow is buried in the grounds – he died in 1702 after a battle with the French. The Parade is also bordered on its northern side by **Ward Theatre**, an attractive pale blue and white building dating from 1911, which hosts many good productions, not least the annual pantomime. Further north is the 74-acre (30-hectare) **National Heroes Park**, with modern monuments dedicated to heroes such as Paul Bogle, as well as the tombs of Marcus Garvey and Norman Manley.

The **uptown** area includes New Kingston, a modern development of hotels, banks, shops and offices. Just west of here is Half Way Tree, a main intersection in the city – where market people coming down from the mountains used to rest on the roots of a huge cottonwood tree. Close to the Half Way Tree intersection is **St Andrew's Parish Church**, which has the island's oldest church registers, dating back to 1666. The Jamaica Tourist Board office is not far from here on Dominica Drive, New Kingston. Just northeast, on Montrose Road, is **Vale Royal**,

Nightlife dazzles in Kingston

a splendid white 17th-century building which is the Prime Minister's residence; the lookout tower on the roof was used to watch movements of ships in the harbour.

There are several worthwhile sights to be visited in the uptown area – such as picturesque Devon House (described below). On Hope Road are the extensive and prettily landscaped grounds surrounding **Kings House**, the official residence of the governor-general – the gardens are open to the public weekdays. Further east is the **University of the West Indies** which sits on the site of the old Mona and Papine sugar estates, and the ruins of the aqueduct and sugar factory are scattered over the campus. The Mona Campus Chapel, near the main gate, was originally an old sugar warehouse – built of stone in 1799 – which has been moved and faithfully reassembled here. By the university campus is the Papine Market, which bustles with life from Thursday to Saturday.

What to See Downtown

◆

AFRICAN CARIBBEAN INSTITUTE

12 Ocean Boulevard

Research into African traditions in Jamaica and the Caribbean is conducted here, and there is a display of arts and crafts; the library includes collections relating to the social and ethnic history of the island.

Open: Monday to Friday 09.00–16.00hrs.

◆◆

INSTITUTE OF JAMAICA

12 East Street

This was founded in the 19th century for the 'encouragement of literature, science and art'. It has the world's largest collection of reference material on the West Indies in the National Library of Jamaica, including some noteworthy lithographic prints of Jamaica and the Americas. Among the documents are the Shark Papers: a ship's log

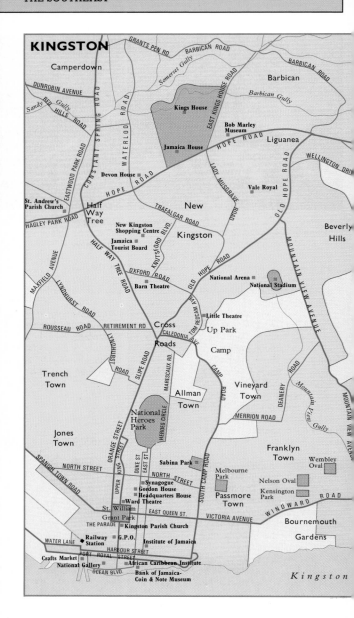

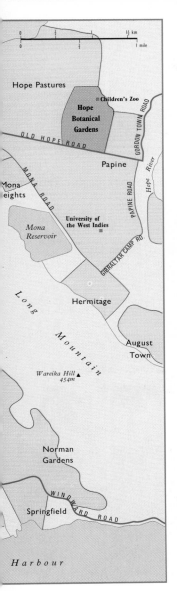

showing evidence of illicit trading which was tossed overboard when the boat was stopped by a British vessel in 1799, and later recovered in the stomach of a shark, leading to the guilty captain's conviction. The complex includes the Natural History Division. The institute hosts educational exhibitions, lectures and art shows.
Open: Monday to Friday 09.00–17.00hrs (Friday 16.00hrs).

◆◆
NATIONAL GALLERY OF JAMAICA
Roy West Building, on the corner of Orange Street and Ocean Boulevard
An outstanding collection of Jamaican art is housed here, from colonial times to an especially exciting display of works from this century. There are sculptures by Edna Manley (wife of Jamaica's second Prime Minister, and mother of another, Michael Manley), including the beautiful *Negro Aroused* (1939). One room is packed with the paintings and sculpture of leading artist Kapo (Mallica Reynolds). There is also a controversial big bronze statue of Bob Marley.
Open: Monday to Saturday 10.00–17.00hrs.

What to See Uptown
◆◆
BOB MARLEY MUSEUM
56 Hope Road
In a 19th-century mansion, flying the Ethiopian flag and with a dreadlocked statue of Marley in front, this museum of

memorabilia and artwork shows the musician's life from his childhood in the ghetto, to fame as the legendary reggae superstar, and then early death from cancer.
Open: Monday, Tuesday, Thursday and Friday 09.30–16.30hrs; Wednesday and Saturday 12.30–15.30hrs.

◆◆◆
DEVON HOUSE
26 Hope Road, at the intersection of Waterloo Road
This elegant classical-style mansion was built in 1881 by one of the first black millionaires in the Caribbean (George Stiebel, who made his money mining gold in Venezuela). It has been beautifully restored and the rooms furnished with period antiques in various historic styles of Jamaica.
Open: Tuesday to Saturday, 09.30–17.00hrs. Sunday 11.00–16.00hrs. The mellow brick stable blocks at the back have been turned into little

shops, selling a fine collection of Jamaican crafts; there is also a tempting cake shop and ice-cream parlour. They surround a garden courtyard where you can sit. Or relax on the Coffee Terrace, with its cool tiles and lovely gingerbread fretwork. There are also two restaurants and shops.
Open: Monday to Saturday; Restaurants every day.

◆◆
HOPE BOTANICAL GARDENS
Old Hope Road, just north of the University
The gardens (which were called the Royal Botanical Gardens after Queen Elizabeth visited them in 1953) were laid out in 1881 on 200 acres (81 hectares) with spacious lawns, ornamental gardens and a lovely Orchid House. You can see many exotic species of plants here; there is also a small zoo and children's funfair.
Open: daily, 06.00–18.00hrs.

Elegant Devon House

Accommodation

Kingston's accommodation ranges from large high-rise hotels, which cater well for business travellers, to small guest houses (and even camping not far outside the city). Unlike the rest of the island, where hotels have lower off-season rates, Kingston hotels charge one rate all year. Although this is the capital city, accommodation is varied and reasonable. Many hotels have lovely views of the mountains. Among the higher-priced is the modern **Jamaica Pegasus Hotel**, 81 Knutsford Boulevard (tel: 926 3690), in New Kingston; the atmosphere is sophisticated but impersonal. It has a wide range of facilities including an attractive pool, good shops, and several restaurants (such as the up-market Talk of the Town on the top floor). The neighbouring **Wyndham New Kingston**, 77 Knutsford Boulevard (tel: 926 5430) is another big tower, smart and spacious, with a similar approach to the Pegasus; it also has excellent facilities, including a large pool. A little more moderately-priced, but also popular with business people is the **Oceana Hotel**, 2 King Street (tel: 922 0990), one of the new waterfront buildings, next to the conference centre and by the harbour; it has good facilities, including a pool. **The Courtleigh**, 31 Trafalgar Road (tel: 926 8174), is a smaller hotel in the northern part of New Kingston, offering reasonable rates. It also has

self-catering apartments, and one of its bars, Mingles, is a lively spot at night. In a similar price bracket, the small **Terra Nova Hotel**, 17 Waterloo Road (tel: 926 9334), lies just north of New Kingston past Devon House. Originally an elegant private house, it is set in lovely gardens with a pool, and has a popular restaurant and nightclub. Not far from here, by the grounds of King House, is the **Mayfair**, 4 West Kings House Close (tel: 926 1610); a good bet for the budget-conscious, the lavish poolside buffet (on Wednesday evening) and barbecue (on Saturday) are firm favourites. Two of the most appealing hotels lie outside the city. South of Kingston Harbour, not far from the airport, is **Morgan's Harbour Hotel**, Port Royal (tel: 924 8464). This comfortable hotel is set in gardens beside the harbour, with splendid views across to Kingston and the mountains behind (the city can be quickly reached by ferry). Apart from a marina, the hotel also offers a range of watersports. Rates are reasonable, especially for rooms without the good views. High on the slopes of the Blue Mountains, about 16 miles (26km) northeast of the city, is the little **Pine Grove Hotel** (tel: 922 8705; the postal address is 62 Duke Street, Kingston). Surrounded by a coffee plantation, it offers a peaceful haven for the budget-conscious in simple rooms and cottages; they have self-catering facilities or you can eat in the dining room (no pool,

THE SOUTHEAST

but the opportunities for hiking are marvellous).

Nightlife and Entertainment
There are several companies offering organised trips all over the island (such as JUTA, 85 Knutsford Boulevard) – the Tourist Board or hotels can give you information. Apart from the guided coach tours, you can also take helicopter excursions (Helitours are based at 120 Main Street, Ocho Rios, tel: 974 2265). If you want to take a boat ride across the harbour, catch the little ferry from the pier near the Crafts Market to Port Royal; there are regular departures through the day, with more on Saturdays and fewer on Sundays. Alternatively, small boats leave the ferry jetty at the Fishermen's Beach in Port Royal for Lime Cay.
Kingston's humming heartbeat continues well into the night, with a variety of nightclubs, discos and bars. Some of the hotels have popular nightspots. For instance, the **Jonkanoo Lounge** at the Wyndham Hotel, is a posh place that has slick nightclub acts, and dancing for the 'mature' crowd. The Jamaica Pegasus Hotel has various evening entertainments, including live jazz in the **Surrey Tavern** on Thursday nights. The Oceana Hotel offers a disco and live entertainment. The **Terra Nova Hotel**'s nightclub attracts an up-market clientele; and **Mingles** at the Courtleigh Hotel is a jolly spot in the evening. (For addresses of hotels see above, under **Accommodation**.)

Illusions, Lane Plaza, 2 South Avenue, is a sophisticated disco where locals come to dance. Another local favourite is **Epiphany**, Spanish Court Plaza, St Lucia Avenue, where you can enjoy reggae (Friday to Sunday only). Near by are two more discos worth trying, also in New Kingston: the **Seawitch**, 69 Knutsford Boulevard, is a popular local place at the end of the week; in **The Club**, 53 Knutsford Boulevard, the young and trendy dance to reggae or disco music, with live performers on Wednesday and Sunday. At Devon House, the **Grog Shoppe** offers exotic rum cocktails and dancing under the stars.
If you are interested in live music, contact the Tourist Board, ask your hotel or consult listings in *The Daily Gleaner*. The **National Stadium**, the **Randy Williams Performance Centre** and the University's **Creative Arts Centre** occasionally put on shows; and entertainment, including reggae, is frequently held at the **centre** by Fort Clarence Beach.
The colourful **Skateland Rolla Disco**, 71/2 Constant Spring Road has a huge rink, and a live band on Wednesday nights.

Theatres
Kingston is the centre of Jamaica's cultural entertainments, and theatres boast a wide variety of shows and concerts. The **Ward Theatre**, North Parade, has excellent dramatic and

musical performances. The **National Pantomime** is a Jamaican institution, held here from Boxing Day to April, offering song and dance, satirical commentaries on current affairs, witty spoofs of historic events – and plenty of audience reaction.

The **Little Theatre**, 4 Tom Redcam Avenue, hosts plays, dance and folk concerts. This is where you can see the brilliant **National Dance Theatre Company** perform innovative dances that draw inspiration from the kaleidoscope of ethnic influences on the island – the absolute acme of Jamaican grace and rhythm. The main season is from mid-July to mid-August, but there is a short series of performances at the end of November and beginning of December. This theatre also hosts an annual season of concerts by Olive Lewin's **Jamaican Folk Singers**, who combine movement with music to provide entertainment that is educational.

The **Barn Theatre**, 5 Oxford Road, is the island's most highly acclaimed theatre company.

Consult the Tourist Board, your hotel or *The Daily Gleaner* for details of classical concerts and other musical events. The University's Creative Arts Centre and the Terra Nova Hotel hold concerts and cultural shows.

Restaurants

Kingston boasts a wide choice of places to eat, from those offering a gourmet menu and

The Ward Theatre

sophisticated ambience to Chinese restaurants and burger bars. Many of the hotels are worth trying, including those mentioned above.

One of Kingston's most renowned restaurants is the **Blue Mountain Inn**, on the Gordon Town road (tel: 927 1700). The setting makes it so spectacular: this 18th-century, colonial coffee plantation house is secluded in a deep valley beside the Hope River. It opens for dinner only, and is expensive (the wine list is good) – but the surroundings make it special.

Norma, 8 Belmont Road (tel: 929 4966), is a garden restaurant frequented by the fashionable, and serving deliciously chic nouvelle cuisine. A classy place at high prices.

At Devon House you can choose from the **Devonshire** (tel: 929 7046), the most sophisticated of its restaurants overlooking the garden courtyard; the informal, inexpensive **Grog Shoppe** (tel: 929 7027) set on the patio and specialising in Jamaican dishes, or the **Coffee Terrace** (tel: 929 7063) which is good for breakfast or tea, but is not open in the evening like the other two.

If you're after *ital* food (vegetarian Rasta food), try **Minnie's Ethiopian Herbal Health Food Restaurant**, 176 Old Hope Road (tel: 927 9207). Minnie used to cook for Bob Marley, and you can sample some tasty, often piquant, vegetarian fare; the Friday night live reggae adds an authentic flavour.

If you fancy a seafood lunch at lower prices than **Morgan's Harbour Hotel**, but with similarly wonderful views across the harbour, try the **Fisherman's Cabin** (no phone) at Port Royal by the Fishermen's Beach.

For a finger-licking-good snack of freshly caught and fried fish, served with festival (crispy fried dumpling) or bammy (fried cassava bread), visit one of the beachside shacks at Hellshire Beach.

Shopping

As you would expect in a capital city, the opportunities for shopping are excellent, and for bargains, too. The **Crafts Market**, by the waterfront on Port Royal Street has the island's largest collection of local crafts – handmade straw and woven goods, wood carvings, embroidery and more unusual items like dried calabashes or yoyos made from cacoon (a large seed from a vine pod). The market is within a large building, but there are also lots of pavement higglers outside. Craft souvenirs may be cheaper here than in the north coast resorts, as higglers often buy goods in Kingston and sell them elsewhere on the island. If you enjoy visiting markets, you can find a variety of everyday items at the bustling **Coronation Market**, on Lower Spanish Town Road, or **Papine Market** by the university campus (both in action at the end of the week).

The pretty little shops behind **Devon House**, 26 Hope Road, where you can browse without being hassled, offer a lovely selection of fine crafts and gifts, including pottery, leather goods, carving, dolls and baskets.

There are several modern shopping plazas in Kingston,

including the **New Kingston Shopping Centre**, 30 Dominica Drive, which has over 30 shops in a smart complex around a courtyard with a splashing fountain and a large, free underground car park; there are some stylish shops here. Another shopping complex worth visiting is **The Springs**, Half Way Tree Road, which has designer boutiques and a good bookshop. There are several shops selling duty-free items around Kingston, such as in the **Mall Plaza**, 20 Constant Spring Road; the **Jamaica Pegasus Hotel** on Knutsford Boulevard also has a duty-free shop. **Dallas 40 Collection**, 30B Constant Spring Road, sells beach and sportswear for men and women; it also does printing and custom work on clothes.

For quality Jamaican art try **Contemporary**, 1 Liguanea Avenue; the **Frame Centre Gallery**, 10 Tangerine Place; **Four Corners Gallery**, 7 West Arcadia Avenue; **Upstairs Downstairs**, 108 Harbour Street; and **Bolivar Gallery** (which also has a bookshop) at the corner of Half Way Tree

and Grove roads.
If you are looking out for reggae records, try one of the music shops (and stalls) in Orange Street or on The Parade.

Sports

Active visitors will find enough to keep them on their toes in Kingston, and spectators can also enjoy a variety of sports. Watersports are centred on Morgan's Harbour Hotel and Marina. From here you can go diving to explore the sunken remains of Port Royal, or snorkelling to see the colourful coral and tropical fishes. Otherwise there are opportunities for waterskiing, windsurfing, sailing and deep-sea fishing. You can also contact the Royal Jamaica Yacht Club, further east along the Palisadoes peninsula beside the harbour, if you wish to charter a boat.
Golf enthusiasts can find two championship courses in the area: the Caymanas Golf Club, lying 10 miles (16km) west of

Traditional costumes in the New Kingston Shopping Centre

THE SOUTHEAST

central Kingston, has a challenging course; Constant Spring Golf Club is set on a hillside north of the city with splendid views.

The larger hotels offer sports facilities such as tennis; the Jamaica Pegasus and Wyndham hotels also have gyms. At the Constant Spring Golf Club you will find tennis, badminton and squash courts, and a pool.

You can watch various equestrian events at Caymanas Park, where polo is played every Thursday and Sunday; you can also have a flutter on the horse-racing at Caymanas Park, on Wednesdays, Saturdays or holidays. Other spectator sports include cricket at Sabina Park, from January to August, or soccer during the autumn and winter.

Events

The capital hosts a multitude of different events through the year. Apart from polo tournaments, show-jumping and horse trials at Caymanas Park, there are also major golf tournaments at Caymanas Golf Club and at Constant Spring Golf Club. The international cricket matches at Sabina Park always draw large audiences. Tennis tournaments are also held in Kingston. The Royal Jamaica Yacht Club organises a regatta in the harbour at the beginning of August as part of the Independence Day celebrations.

The University of the West Indies has a carnival in February, while the Orange Carnival and Jamaica Carnival both take place in April. There are events, shows and competitions of every description during **Festival!** in July, leading up to the celebrations for Independence Day on 6 August which include a street parade and grand gala. Oktoberfest is a festival with a German theme, in October. You can hear live reggae, soca and pop performed by top artists from Jamaica and abroad, at the big Superjam music festival held in late December.

Flower-lovers can enjoy shows put on by the **Jamaica Orchid Society** at the end of March and beginning of October. The St Elizabeth Horticultural

Hot stuff: Jamaican limbo

Society Flower Show in late April is the largest in the Caribbean.
Contact the Tourist Board for information on events.

Beaches

Lying offshore, south of Kingston Harbour, is **Lime Cay** – a pretty coral islet with a pale sandy beach, ideal for swimming, snorkelling or picnicking. It can be reached by a small boat from the jetty at the Fishermen's Beach, Port Royal.

Other beaches to try are on the Hellshire coast southwest of the city. **Fort Clarence** is a sandy beach with changing facilities, as well as an entertainment centre which holds live music shows. A little further down the coast is **Hellshire Beach**, a fine stretch of sand popular with locals. At the back of the beach are bamboo shacks where women fry fresh fish and bammy – the wafting smells are quite irresistible.

There are two other sandy beaches in the southeast area that are worth a visit if you are passing; both are very remote and unspoilt. **Holland Bay** lies on the little road to Morant Point Lighthouse, on the southeastern tip of the island (about 48 miles (76km) east of Kingston); this white-sand beach is bordered by cliffs, with sugar cane plantations and coconut palms spread over the flat plain behind. Near the fishing hamlet of Rocky Point is **Jackson Bay** (about 48 miles (76km) southwest of Kingston).

WHAT ELSE TO SEE IN THE SOUTHEAST

◆
BATH

There is little to show that this was a fashionable watering place in the 18th century, as it is now just a small, quiet farming community, although the reputed therapeutic value of the hot springs continues to attract visitors. The springs were discovered 300 years ago, after a runaway slave claimed that bathing in the waters had cured chronic ulcers on his legs. The present Bath Fountain mineral spa is in a simple, rather run-down building which was originally opened in 1747, and lies just outside the town. The water emerges from the rocks at two different temperatures, which is mixed to give hot baths; the high lime and sulphur content is regarded as beneficial for treating rheumatic ailments and skin diseases. You can partake of the waters in several ways.
Open: daily.

In the centre of town are the Botanical Gardens, the only other evidence of Bath's distinguished past, although they too are just a shadow of their former splendour, especially since Hurricane Gilbert caused extensive damage here. In one corner are the offspring of the original breadfruit brought from Tahiti by Captain Bligh of the *Bounty*. The gardens are closed at present and are due to be reconstructed but you can in fact see them quite easily.

THE SOUTHEAST

◆◆◆
THE BLUE MOUNTAINS

This ridge of magnificent peaks dominates the eastern end of the island; many soar over 6,000 feet (1,829m), and the rounded Blue Mountain Peak reaches 7,402 feet (2,256m) – the highest point on the island. The cool climate here averages 65°F (18°C) during the day. The upper reaches are often swathed in swirling mist by mid-morning, which gives them a hazy blue cast from a distance. Whichever way you approach the mountains, the route will be tortuous and often rough – and to get to the summit involves a long, strenuous hike up a steep track. The southern slopes are more accessible than those on the Portland side of the ridge, to the north, where torrential rainfall has deterred people from clearing the rugged terrain of its densely tangled tropical forests in order to settle and use the land, as has happened in parts of the south side, especially the area close to Kingston. The landscapes and panoramas are inspirational.

Gordon Town lies 1,200 feet (366m) up in the Hope River valley, a few miles northeast of Kingston, and nestles in a profusion of colourful plants. Many of the plants found here are descendants of those imported for a long-vanished botanical garden, but which have remained an important part of the island flora of Jamaica – such as hibiscus, oleander, jasmine, azalea, magnolia and cassia. The winding road climbs the mountain sides, heading east towards **Guava Ridge**. Many of the houses here are surrounded by patches of vegetables and fruit, from yams to asparagus, banana palms to strawberry plants. This is where most of Kingston's fresh produce comes from: towards the end of the week, the smallholders head towards the city to sell their wares in one of the markets. This way of life has hardly changed in 150 years, since the emancipated slaves originally settled on this free land. Further along you pass **'World's End'**, a distillery run by the Scot Ian Sangster; you can tour the factory and taste the rum and liqueurs produced under the 'Sangster's Old Jamaica' label.

Going north from Guava Ridge, a few miles past the Pine Grove Hotel, is the riverside forestry station of **Clydesdale**. It used to be a coffee plantation – you can still see an old waterwheel and coffee-drying barbecues – but now there are stretches of young conifer trees. Near by is the **Cinchona Botanical Gardens**, in a stunning setting high on a mountain ridge that drops steeply from 5,500 to 4,500 feet (1,670 to 1,370m) with three river valleys far below. It was originally established as a cinchona and Assam tea plantation in 1868 – cinchona is a tree from whose bark quinine is obtained – but in the face of large-scale competition from India, it failed.

This region produces coffee

Blue Mountain Peak

that is renowned for its flavour throughout the world. Several old plantation Great Houses remain, mostly built during the boom period of the early 19th century – the coffee plantations themselves have declined since then. To the northwest of Cinchona is **Silver Hill**, with one of the Blue Mountains' few coffee factories (another is near Mavis Bank; visitors are welcome at both factories).

West of Silver Hill lies **Hollywell Park**, where the mountain slopes around Hardwar Gap are covered in a 300-acre (120-hectare) forest reserve. Thatched rondavels offer shelter for picnickers, necessary as it is a misty area with heavy rainfall – but the peaceful surroundings and vistas of Kingston are splendid. It is a great place for hiking, with miles of trails.

Just a couple of miles southeast is **Newcastle** (18 miles (29km) northeast of Kingston), a training camp for the Jamaica Defence Force set on a mountain-side, at around 4,000 feet (1,219m) overlooking the Mammee River valley.

It was established in 1841 as a hill station for the British troops, at a time when diseases like yellow fever took a fatal toll at low altitudes. Visitors can use the Sergeant's Mess and bar.

You have to be determined and fit to make it to the top of the **Blue Mountain Peak**. From Mavis Bank (16 miles (26km) east of Kingston), it is a tough climb up a rough track, which takes at least three hours. The route takes you through thick forest until, at around 5,500 feet (1,676m), open woodland takes over. The peaks are often cloaked in mist from mid-morning to around 18.00hrs, which gives the scenery a rather other-worldly look. The spectacular isolation, and breathtaking views over the whole island make the climb worthwhile. On a clear day, Cuba can be seen in the distance to the north. The classic hike starts at 02.00 or 03.00hrs to reach the peak in time for a sensational sunrise. A practical point: climbers need strong, comfortable shoes and warm clothes. The magic of the Blue Mountains is better appreciated if you give yourself two days to explore, and stay overnight (or longer). There is a variety of modest accommodation available in the area. The Tourist Board provides information. Otherwise, for details of cabins, rooms, camping and hikes (guided or on your own, from half a day to five-day backpacking treks), contact Peter Bentley, Maya Lodge, PO Box 216, Kingston 7 (tel: 927 2097). This includes information on cabins or camping at Clydesdale and Hollywell, but for log cabins here you can also contact the Forestry Department, 173 Constant Spring Road, Kingston (tel: 924 2667). The Jamaica Defence Force has cottages to rent at Cinchona and Newcastle – details from Newcastle Hill Sta 1T (tel: 944 8230). The Pine Grove Hotel is listed under Kingston's Accommodation. Whitfield Hall is a hostel in an old coffee plantation house, set at 4,200 feet (1,280m) not far from the Blue Mountain Peak. There is also a simple cottage with cooking facilities on the summit (ask the Tourist Board).

◆
MORANT BAY

This tiny, quiet town on the south coast – 32 miles (51km) east of Kingston – is of interest because this is where the slaves' Morant Bay Rebellion took place in 1865. A statue of Paul Bogle, the Baptist preacher who led the rebellion, stands in the town square by the courthouse. The statue was created by Edna Manley, the Jamaican sculptor. Morant Bay's original courthouse burnt down during the rebellion, and Bogle was hanged inside the gutted building – the present courthouse is a reconstruction.

◆
OLD HARBOUR

Lying on the coastal plain, not far from the sea (about 24 miles (38km) west of Kingston), this is a typical local town. It has a Victorian clock tower near the centre, which, unlike many on the island, tells the right time. Just to the north is the Little Ascot Race Course. Nearly two miles (3km) northwest of the town are the ruins of Colbeck Castle. This stone mansion, with slave quarters underground, is thought to have been built in the late 17th century by an unpopular Englishman, Colonel John Colbeck, and fortified as a protection against Maroons or French invaders.

◆◆◆
PORT ROYAL

The quiet atmosphere of this fishing village, at the entrance to Kingston Harbour, belies its glittering (if dissolute) past. In the 17th century it became the infamous lair of the swashbuckling buccaneers, who squandered their ill-gotten loot on wine (or rum), and wild times. Port Royal was also important in the 18th century as the regional headquarters of the British Royal Navy. Recognising its strategic importance, the English built a fort here within a year of their capture of Jamaica in 1655. Port Royal gained its name in 1662, at the time of the Restoration in England; and the fort was christened Fort Charles, in honour of King Charles II.

A settlement quickly sprung up around the fort; although the site was poor for the development of a town, it had the great advantages of a magnificent harbour and deep anchorage alongside. It became a base for trade and the buccaneers' attacks on Spanish ships and ports (at first encouraged by the English) – which brought increasing riches to Port Royal. In Port Royal's heyday, Spanish gold and silver were the coinage used here.

The town was ringed by six fortresses, and by 1688 was jam-packed with some 1,200 houses (most were four storeys high – with rents equally high); it had thousands of inhabitants. There was a proliferation of taverns and rum shops, which numbered one for every 10 residents, as well as brothels, gaming houses and goldsmiths. The legendary reprobate and buccaneer, Henry Morgan, was very much at home here.

Perhaps it was appropriate that the town should meet a violent and dramatic end, like many of its inhabitants. Certainly many believed it was divine retribution when an earthquake struck it down in 1692. About 2,000 lives were lost as buildings collapsed in clouds of dust and great fissures swallowed them. In a matter of minutes, two-thirds of Port Royal had plunged beneath the sea; devastation and chaos reigned amid the horrifying carnage.

Rebuilding started, trade was revived, but Port Royal suffered a series of further

Passing time in Port Royal . . .

THE SOUTHEAST

blows – first a fire reduced the town to ashes in 1704, then the following 47 years saw it hit by five ferocious hurricanes. Port Royal refused to die, but these disasters helped ensure that it never recovered the character of its days of infamy and fortune. Kingston, across the harbour, replaced Port Royal as the island's chief trading centre.

During the 18th century, the Caribbean was the scene of continuous maritime conflict between the British, French and Spanish. Port Royal was increasingly used by the Royal Navy, and emerged as the most important British naval station in the Caribbean, until it literally went out in a blaze of glory, ravaged by a fire in 1815. The naval dockyard was closed in 1905.

As you approach Port Royal today, you pass a long red-brick wall which enclosed the old naval dockyard – today Morgan's Harbour Hotel lies on the site. From here you can look across to the sinister saltmarsh of Gallows Point, where many pirates met their end. Among these was 'Calico Jack' Rackham, whose body was then squeezed into an iron frame and strung up as a gruesome deterrent to others, on a sandy cay off Port Royal which still bears his name. The sunken city adds an intriguing dimension to this historic site – with legends of sunken treasure – and some claim to have heard the eerie tolling of underwater church bells on stormy days.

Towards the far end of Port Royal – and at some distance from its original position right on the sea – is **Fort Charles**. This is one of the oldest and best-preserved of Jamaica's many forts. It dates from 1656, although repairs and additions changed it considerably over the years. On one side you can see the raised wooden platform where Nelson watched anxiously for a French invasion that never came – today called Nelson's Quarterdeck.

To the south is the **Victoria and Albert Battery**, a defensive structure built in 1888 along with the Royal Artillery Store at one end, which is better known as the Giddy House, since it became tilted at a rakish angle in the 1907 earthquake. The origin of its nickname is obvious if you try walking inside. Just north of the parade ground is the long impressive **Old Naval Hospital**, built in 1819. The building is of interest as one of the earliest to be constructed of prefabricated cast-iron sections brought out from England. It houses the **Archaeological Museum**, which has an interesting display of objects recovered from the sunken city – such as candelabra, bottles, silver, bone wig curlers and ivory articles.

Not far from the entrance breach in the old walls around Port Royal, lies **St Peter's Church**. This building dates from 1725, and inside there is a striking organ loft, erected in 1743, with palm-leaf carvings and elaborate mouldings. Other features from this period include the altar which has attractive railings, and brass candelabrum. Some of the memorials give a good picture of life (or death) in the 18th and 19th centuries. In the churchyard lies the tomb of Louis Galdy who had an extraordinary escape in the earthquake when the ground opened to swallow him – and then spat him out again into the sea.

Nearby is the village itself, where little terraced houses with verandas line the small streets behind the Fisherman's Beach. There is a jetty here where the connecting ferry to Kingston arrives and boats go to Lime Cay.

Port Royal has other historic sites and buildings – such as the 19th-century military hospital beside the church and the old jail (parts of which probably predate the 1692 earthquake) – so it is worth looking at a map which shows details of these. Fort Charles and other sights open Monday to Saturday, 10.00 to 17.00hrs. The small passenger ferry from Kingston runs several times throughout the day; otherwise it is about 14 miles (22km) from downtown Kingston by road.

◆◆◆
SPANISH TOWN

Founded by a son of Christopher Columbus, this was the capital of Jamaica for over 300 years. Most of the original Spanish buildings were destroyed by the English in a fit of pique, when they arrived in 1655 to find the town empty and bare of booty, the Spaniards having fled with their valuables. It continued to be the colonial capital under the British – who gave it its present name – until 1872.

In the centre of this sizeable town is a serene and graceful **square** (The Park), first set out by the Spanish. The well-kept central garden is dominated by elegant royal palms, and bordered by splendid Georgian buildings. On one side sits the old British **House of Assembly**, dating from 1762 and now housing the local parish council offices. It is a red-brick building with a superb shady colonnade running along its length and a pillared wooden balcony above. Opposite lies **King's House** (also built in 1762) which was the residence of the island's governor; in 1925 it was gutted by fire, but the impressive façade with its grand portico remain to bear witness that this was considered the finest governor's residence in the British Colonies. It has been partially restored, and houses the Jamaica People's **Museum of Craft and Technology**, a folk museum which has cultural displays and a varied collection of historic relics, some found on the property – everything from a variety of home furnishings to a carriage, a pimento fanner, and a village store.

Open: daily 10.00–17.00hrs.

On the south side of the square, the large red-brick **Courthouse** (1819) suffered the same fate as King's House and was devastated by a fire a few years ago. Opposite is a classically grand white-stucco structure, in the centre of which is the **Rodney Memorial**, honouring Admiral Rodney who saved the island from invasion by the French in 1782 (not in Roman times, as the statue's clothing suggests). There are some other graceful old buildings in the area around the square.

A few blocks south on Barrett Street is the **Cathedral of St Jago de la Vega** (also called the Cathedral Church of St James). The present building was erected in 1714, and it is the second oldest building on the island (after Fort Charles at Port Royal). It is an attractive brick church built in the form of a cross, set in tranquil

walled gardens, the brick tower (added in 1831) is crowned by an appealing white wood spire with a pointed red shingle roof. It contains several memorials to notable figures in Jamaican history.

Spanish Town lies about 14 miles (22km) west of downtown Kingston. Almost three miles (5km) east of Spanish Town, beside the main road to Kingston, is the **White Marl Arawak Museum** in a polygonal building with a shingle roof, whose design was inspired by a *caneye*, a traditional Arawak Indian dwelling. Jamaica's main collection of Arawak artefacts is housed here.

Open: Monday to Saturday 10.00–17.00hrs.

Deep in the hills about 10 miles (16km) northwest of Spanish Town (along a small road), just past Guanaboa Vale, is the **Mountain Valley cave**. Ask a local to guide you along a rough path to this ancient cave which contains Arawak drawings. Mostly on flat limestone surfaces, there are designs of birds, turtles and hunters.

Spanish Town

THE SOUTHWEST

Blue skies at Black River

This area includes the parishes of Manchester and Clarendon, lying in the most westerly part of the county of Middlesex, together with the parish of St Elizabeth and the southern half of Westmoreland, both lying to the south of the county of Cornwall. Mandeville is the largest town, set in the cool highlands. There are no resorts aimed at mass tourism – although there are a few little places along the coast where small hotels or simple guest houses can be found, such as Treasure Beach and Black River. Environmentalists are fighting to keep the developers at bay, as it is the unspoilt, natural appeal of the area that gives it such great charm.

There are wooded pastures on the rolling hillsides in the area around Mandeville.

Manchester's mountain plateau has slopes of jungle further north. And the mountains stretch westwards along the spectacular southern edge of Cockpit Country, where the peaks and deep valleys are cloaked in forest.

South of Mandeville, the high hills continue right down to the coast, where they are covered in bush and scrub, with spiky aloe plants and a few sabal thatch palms, their heads of thick fronds rising above the bush. The ridge of the rocky Santa Cruz Mountains runs northwest from the coast near here, falling to a wide valley west of Mandeville, and the coastal plain on the other side. Much of the landscape looks parched in this area, especially around Treasure Beach. It is a typical hot, still savannah of golden grass.

THE SOUTHWEST

There are fewer rivers in this area, but one of them is the Black River, and its tributaries, which pass through green valleys to the flat wetlands and mangrove swamps on the coast – where there is a wealth of wildlife – northwest of Treasure Beach. There are also rivers flowing down from the mountains in the north to the plains around Savanna-la-Mar in the west. On this flat coastal plain there are extensive sugar plantations, as well as inland in St Elizabeth, with citrus groves towards the east.

In striking contrast to this agricultural landscape are the open-cast bauxite mines in the Manchester area.

Along the coast are scattered quiet little fishing settlements – the eastern parts of the coast are most sparsely inhabited, accessible only by a few narrow roads. The coast itself boasts some pretty beaches; they may lack the finesse of some of those along the north, but they have the advantage of being quite unspoilt and often deserted.

This is not the swish Jamaica of the tourist brochures, but a haven for those who really want to get away from it all.

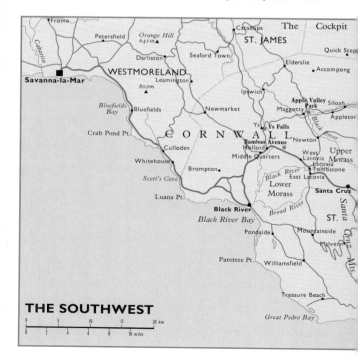

THE SOUTHWEST

♦♦♦
BLACK RIVER

On a sheltered bay at the mouth of the Black River, this charming fishing town was once a major exporter of logwood, a tree from which indigo dye was produced until synthetic means were found to manufacture it. Its days of wealth and prominence as a port have long gone – even the once-popular mineral spa just outside town has been abandoned (although there are rumours of redevelopment). There are many Georgian gingerbread-style houses, especially along the main sea-road going west out of the centre. Some of these wooden buildings obviously once had an elegant demeanour, but have now entered a rickety and creaky old age – though still picturesque.

Around the centre, which lies beside the sea, are some old cream-painted clapboard houses, with overhanging upper storeys supported by columns over the street, where there are shops and a few bars. By the main road junction is St John's Parish Church. One of the curates, who is buried here, was a distant relative of William Shakespeare. The

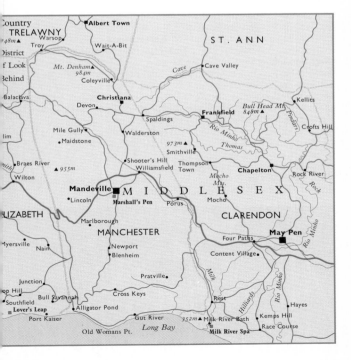

little town explodes with colour and activity on Friday and Saturday, when the market takes place.

You can take a boat trip along the Black River from the road bridge on the east side of town, to look at the wildlife and scenery of the flat swamplands stretching from the coast inland. This area around Black River is a splash of green in the otherwise dry savannah landscapes along the coast.

Accommodation

The following offer accommodation on the coast for the budget-minded. The **Port of Call Hotel** (tel: 965 2360) lies behind Crane Beach, close to Black River. The large open bar room has a long veranda overlooking the beach. The **Waterloo Guest House** (tel: 965 2278) is in a historic 150-year-old gingerbread house with decorative fretwork around the upper veranda and old patterned tiles on the floors. Old fashioned and quite basic, it has a well-kept, homely appeal and much character. Prices are very low. Northeast of Black River, around 13 miles (21km) away,

is the small **South Sea View Guest House** (no phone) at Whitehouse. This modern villa is set by the sea, with steps down to bathe in a rocky cove – they are also building a pool. It offers modest but comfortable accommodation. A little further up the coast is another small guest house, **Natania's** (no phone) at Little Culloden. Stylish and well-kept, with a friendly atmosphere, there are attractive gardens leading down to the rocky coast, where you can bathe; there are watersports available here, and a sandy beach at the nearby Cotton Tree Beach Park.

Restaurants

Natania's Guest House has a good seafood restaurant. The dining-room at the Waterloo Guest House is popular for good value home-style meals. The South Sea View Guest House serves tasty Jamaican dishes. And the Port of Call Hotel is also worth trying.

A rickety reminder of Black River's past grandeur

◆◆◆
MANDEVILLE

This calm, rather genteel town is set inland at 2,000 feet (609m) where the clear mountain air and cooler temperatures used to attract British colonists on leave from hot, sticky Kingston. When the British colonial days were over and the holiday emphasis shifted to the beaches, Mandeville's popularity as a resort declined. But this is still a well-heeled and expanding town, largely thanks to the bauxite industry of the region and also because it is the area's agricultural centre for fruit and vegetables.

The town is scattered over green hillsides, surrounded by pastures bounded by drystone walls and leafy woods. Mandeville was established in 1814, when the parish was named after the Jamaican governor, the Duke of Manchester, and the town after his son, Lord Mandeville. And it soon became a playground for European gentry. Today the town is well-kept and orderly – it boasts no slums. The centre lies around a square with a traditional green; beside it sits the Georgian **courthouse**, built by slaves from limestone blocks, and the stone **Manchester Parish Church**, also dating from 1820. The busy market has stalls in front of the church.

One of the most imposing mansions in Mandeville is the octagonal hilltop home built by an ex-mayor. The outdoor swimming pool flows under the walls into a pond in the living room; outside exotic birds hang in cages by the fountain shaped like a map of Jamaica (visits can be arranged – ask your hotel).

An enjoyable visit to make here is to **Mrs Stephenson's Garden**. Carmen Stephenson has won countless prizes over the years for her flowers at the annual Horticultural Show. Her neat garden has orchids in a paintbox of colours, as well as shiny red anthuriums and citrus trees. (Her house is off New Green Road – ask your hotel or the local Tourist Board for details.) You could also enjoy the exotic blooms and colourful foliage on show at the **Paul Cross Nursery** (Manchester Road) which is run by a priest. Finding the **1907 Gallery**, Caledonia Meadows, is well worth the effort. This bar has an eclectic display of antiques and other interesting collectables which are for sale.

Among the many big colonial houses around Mandeville, Marshall's Pen (page 100) is outstanding.

There are several factories a few miles northeast to which tours can be arranged – including the **Pickapeppa Factory** at Shooter's Hill, where the popular piquant sauce is made. Among other suggested tours is the local bammy factory, where they make this Jamaican Cassava bread.

For information on Mandeville and the southern area of Jamaica contact the local Tourist Board at 21 Ward Avenue or Diana McIntyre-Pike at the Astra Hotel (see

Mandeville courthouse

The **Mandeville Hotel** (tel: 962 2138) is larger, and this pleasant place is run by the McIntyre clan, including Diana's parents. There are suites with kitchens, a pool surrounded by a terrace and gardens, and a room for occasional entertainment. Diana McIntyre-Pike also runs a bed and breakfast programme in private homes and guest houses in the area. This scheme is very good value; you can stay in places with character and obtain a genuine taste of Jamaica.

below). This dynamic woman is dedicated to 'community tourism' and has a wealth of information at her polished finger tips. She is always eager to give visitors a whirlwind tour if she has time in her hectic schedule – which includes running her hotel, enthusiastically promoting the area, and fighting to ensure the development of tourism will not harm the environment or its natural character. Mandeville lies in the heart of Jamaica, about 70 miles (112km) from both Montego Bay and Ocho Rios, about 60 miles (96km) from Kingston, and within easy reach of the south.

Accommodation
There are two main hotels in Mandeville, both offering budget prices. The **Astra Hotel** (tel: 962 3265) is a small inn with an intimate atmosphere. It has a cosy pub-bar, small pool and sauna; some rooms have kitchenettes. There is an information centre at the hotel.

Nightlife and Entertainment
There are no extensive tour lists as in the main resorts. But the Astra Hotel and Mandeville Hotel can arrange trips in the area or further afield. Otherwise contact the local Tourist Board office. Walking and birdwatching tours are popular here. The main boat trip in the area is the **Black River Safari** from the coast to the southwest. Mandeville is a quiet town, and does not have a great deal of choice to offer after dark. There are several bars, including the intimate **Revival Room Pub** at the Astra Hotel. **Bill Laurie's Steak House** has the right ambience for a serene evening. The Mandeville Hotel sometimes puts on entertainment or a disco. **Traks**, in the Mandeville Shopping Plaza, is the town's liveliest nightspot. Otherwise **Planet**, Perth Road, has music and dancing.

Restaurants

For home-style food in an informal setting with good service, try the **Astra Hotel** or the **Mandeville Hotel**. Bill Laurie's cook is carrying on his tradition, following his death, at his **Steak House**, Bloomfield Gardens (tel: 962 3116), in a characterful old building with superb views. The **Den**, Caledonia Road (tel: 962 3603), has a shady beer garden and serves delicious, reasonably-priced Jamaican dishes. If you want to go Chinese, try the **International**, Manchester Road (tel: 962 0527).

Shopping

Mandeville has several modern shopping plazas; the main one is the **Manchester Shopping Centre**, Caledonia Road, where you will find **Craft Things Jamaican** selling local handicrafts. Other shopping centres include the **Grove Court**, **Willowgate** and **Caledonia**. The **SWA Craft Centre** (7 North Crescent) is a community project to train girls who have just left school. They produce a black version of Cabbage Patch dolls, pretty embroidery, and tasty Jamaican cookies. The colourful **market** is on one side of Mandeville Square and operates from Monday to Saturday.

Sport

Mandeville boasts Jamaica's oldest golf club: the **Manchester Club** has a nine-green (18-tee) golf course as well as tennis and billiards. Sports can be arranged through your hotel. **John Nightingale**, Perth Road, offers horse-riding – in the perfect countryside for this sport – otherwise ask the **Dalkeith Riding Stables**.

Events

The **Manchester Horticultural Society Show** is held here in May. The **Jamaica Horse Association's Mandeville Show** and the **Manchester Golf Week** are both in July. The **All-Jamaica Hardcourt Tennis Championship** is in August.

The Manchester Golf Club

THE SOUTHWEST

◆◆◆
TREASURE BEACH

Serene, secluded, tranquil and unspoilt, Treasure Beach has an away-from-it-all charm which is hard to beat. Life here is centred on the beaches. The main one is Frenchman's Bay, a curving beach of dark sand, fringed by a few palms. Set in gardens on the dunes behind is a hotel and several villas with rooms to rent. Colourful fishing canoes on the beach have names like Love Bird, Dandy Girl and Inner City. A few Rastas, hippies and visitors sit chatting in one of the palm-thatched bars along the beach, and a group of local boys play football. The atmosphere is seriously relaxed. The undertow on this beach can be rather tricky, so take care when swimming. The smaller sandy beach next to this one – Calabash Bay – is safer for bathing. Between the cliffs and rocky points along this coast, there are other unspoilt sandy coves – some have flat reefs lying just offshore which makes swimming difficult, but reef-walking is a popular pastime to look at the marine life (you may even be lucky enough to see turtles).

Natural living is what Treasure Beach is all about – and that means few facilities. There are a couple of tiny shops selling basic necessities – and a simple supermarket at Great Bay, a fishing community just along the coast to the southeast. If you want a better range of shops (a bank or telephone), Black River is the nearest place; there is also a market at the end of the week. You can buy fish from the fishermen at Treasure Beach; it is best not to approach them when they have just come in, cold and tired, but buy a fisherman a drink one evening and make arrangements in advance. Transport and communication is very difficult here – buses are few and erratic – so arrange transport to the airport in good time (if you decide you can bear to leave). There is a little snack bar, the Jerk Pit, where you can hire bicycles.

A leisurely life in idyllic surroundings is the prize to be found on Treasure Beach

Accommodation

The **Treasure Beach Hotel** (office in Black River, tel: 965 2305) has sparkling white-painted buildings set amid flowery landscaped gardens on a hillock behind the beach, and the budget prices make it good value. There is a good variety of rooms and villas in this area, especially for the budget-conscious. The **Four Ms Cottage** (no phone) is a homely guest house run by the inestimable Effie Campbell. The **Siwind** guest house (no phone) overlooks the sea with a private sandy cove. **Treasure Point Villa** (tel: 965 2536 Jamaica number or 302-539-6198 US number) is a smart, comfortable house by Calabash Bay, with a pool on the terrace. **Sparkling Waters** (203-621-4908 US number) is a pretty villa overlooking the sea with a pool. **Nuestra Casa** (no phone) is a comfortable house where a charming northern English landlady lets a room. For information on these and other guest houses, villas and rooms in Treasure Beach, contact the Tourist Board office in Mandeville. Many visitors just turn up at Treasure Beach and find a room on the spot.

Restaurants

The **Yabba** restaurant at the Treasure Beach Hotel serves tasty dishes in attractive surroundings. The **Sea Crab** (no phone) at nearby Great Bay is a simple restaurant and bar, offering delicious specialities like lobster at reasonable prices.

WHAT ELSE TO SEE IN THE SOUTHWEST

◆

ALLIGATOR POND

Set on the coast 22 miles (35km) south of Mandeville, with mountains behind, there are fishing shacks, and a couple of bars behind the greyish-sand beach, where local boys surf on planks of wood. The village has an early-morning fish market. A rough dirt track follows the coast east (and becomes more impassable towards Milk River Bath, 28 miles (29km) along the coast). Around Long Bay is a dark sand beach, backed by slopes of cacti-strewn rocks and scrub. Gut River is a pretty little place (between Alligator Pond and Milk River Bath); it is totally unspoilt and peaceful, with a few fishing canoes drawn up on the beach. Near by is God's Well, a 160 foot (49m)-deep limestone sinkhole with clear turquoise water.

◆◆

THE APPLETON ESTATE RUM DISTILLERY

This is the oldest and biggest distillery in Jamaica, dating back around 250 years. The estate lies deep in the interior, about 27 miles (43km) northwest of Mandeville, splendidly set in a flat green valley beside Black River, which is covered in an extensive sea of sugar cane fields. The modern reception area is in a plantation-house style, and has a bar and souvenir shop for you to taste and buy the goodies. There are piles of burnt sugar cane beside the factory yard (the fields are burnt before harvesting, to make cutting the cane easier); and a smell of toffee and molasses pervades the air. There is a short tour of the distillery, which begins by showing visitors an old press drawn by a donkey. Methods for extracting the juice are more efficient (and less hard work) now. A popular way to visit the Appleton Distillery is on the Appleton Estate Express from Montego Bay which includes a buffet lunch and other diversions on the way.

Open: Monday to Saturday, 09.00–17.00hrs.

◆◆
APPLE VALLEY PARK

This picturesque leisure park is at Maggotty, a village on the banks of the Black River (about three miles (5km) west of Appleton). The village is much prettier than its name suggests. The entrance to the recently opened Apple Valley Park, Farm and Cultural Centre is opposite a 'sweet bread' shop run by the same people. The park covers 465 acres (188 hectares) of unspoilt countryside, and visitors may walk through the tropical forest full of colourful birds to see the black River Gorge with its cascading waterfalls, or picnic in a grove of coconut palms. Attractions include a canoe ride down river, pedalo rides on one of the ponds, fishing for red snapper, silver perch and carp (which can be cooked and eaten here) or a tour up to

the Maroon village of Accompong in Cockpit Country. The park also offers a variety of entertainments such as concerts or shows, and films on Sunday evenings. There is a restaurant serving Jamaican dishes and accommodation is offered in a guest house by the river, in a hilltop Great House, or camping (tents are available). For information contact Lucille and Patrick Lee, Sweet Bakery, PO Box 22, Maggotty, St Elizabeth.

◆◆◆
BLACK RIVER SAFARI

The Black River is Jamaica's longest, and a tranquil one and a half hour boat trip takes you along the river through part of the island's most extensive wetland. The guide, Charles Swaby, is an expert on the history, flora, fauna and delicate ecological balance of the area, which makes it a fascinating trip. There are dense mangrove thickets along the banks, putting down tangles of roots into the river; pancake water lilies and floating water hyacinths – which bloom bluey-mauve in spring – carpet the water. You may sometimes see fires smoking in the surrounding wetlands as the peaty soil gives off methane gas, which ignites spontaneously; the vegetation grows so quickly it soon looks green again. The peat soil makes the river water look black, although it is actually crystal clear.

The birdlife along the river is a delight. Four ospreys (sea eagles) live here – there are

Speeding along Black River

only six in the UK – and they can sometimes be seen hovering overhead ready to pounce on a fish. There are also several varieties of heron, and delicate jacana birds walking on the waterlilies. When it starts getting hot, crocodiles bask in their favourite spots along the water's edge. Fishermen still use traditional methods of catching fish with conical funnel-shaped traps woven of split bamboo – this design originally came from Africa. They are baited and laid in the water, and the spot is marked with the fisherman's individual sign, such as a particular knot tied in a bullrush.

The boat leaves from by the road bridge on the east side of Black River, 43 miles (69km) southwest of Mandeville. South Coast Safaris can also arrange other trips, including coastal wetland tours, photographic safaris, birdwatching and wildlife tours, fishing trips and canoe or rowing boat rentals. The Black River Safari boat tour runs four times a day; if you are most interested in the birdlife go at 09.00 or 16.00hrs; to see crocodiles go at 11.00 or 14.00hrs.

Bluefields to Scott's Cove

A tranquil unspoilt stretch of coast lying eight to 20 miles (13km to 32km) northwest of Black River. It is worth exploring the south coast to find your own deserted beaches. Before Scott's Cove a dirt track leads off the main road to **Fonthill Beach** (by a sign that says 'Fonthill Private Property – Wildlife Sanctuary'). This is a tiny cove of silvery sand with clear aquamarine waters bathing the reef. **Scott's Cove** is a delightful rocky cove and creek, where a river runs into the sea. Fishermen moor their traditional dugout canoes in the creek. The freshly caught fish are sold with bammy at roadside stalls. The wafting aroma is mouthwatering. A little further on is the small settlement of Whitehouse, and just past here is the **Cotton Tree Beach Park**. A stretch of silver sand is backed by a garden with picnic tables and a bar serving snacks. There are swings for children and watersports are available. The beach is shallow, and the reef lies close to the shore, so it is not easy for swimming – which would be better from the neighbouring rocky coves – but the clear, calm sea makes the beach a good place for children to paddle.

The scenery becomes more green and wooded along the coast road here – especially approaching **Bluefields**, which is a very picturesque area. It was from Bluefields Bay that Henry Morgan and his fleet sailed to sack Panama in 1670. It is a relaxing spot with very few people. An old double-decker bus and boat serve as a jerk pork and snack bar. There are splendid drives up into the mountains inland, with destinations such as the sleepy market and tobacco-growing town of Darliston.

◆
LOVER'S LEAP
Where the Santa Cruz Mountains meet the coast, this escarpment plunges 1,500 feet (457m) directly down to the greeny-blue sea below. There is a lighthouse at the top, the views along the coast are wonderful, but looking down the sheer cliffs is dizzying.

◆◆◆
MARSHALL'S PEN
This splendid 18th-century Great House used to be a 3,740-acre (1,513-hectare) coffee estate. Now it is a 300-acre (121-hectare) cattle farm set amid rolling green hills, with fields surrounded by drystone walls and woods. The house is mostly built of wood and furnished with many beautiful antiques and *objets d'art* both Jamaican and English, including a fine 17th-century chair. The house is almost like a museum, but very personal because it is a private home. The surrounding gardens are charming and there are also the terraces on which the coffee beans were dried (called barbecues). It is a magnificent area for walking and birdwatching. The house is on the outskirts of Mandeville, and tours can be arranged through the Astra or Mandeville hotels.

A dizzy plunge: Lover's Leap

Lover's Leap lighthouse

miraculous cure, his owner promised no more punishment if he showed him where it was. On his death, the owner willed the property to the government for the benefit of the people. The mineral spring water is reputed to be the most radioactive in the world, and recommended for rheumatism, eczema, and numerous other complaints. There is a simple bath building, where locals sit discussing their ailments while waiting for their healing baths. There is also an outdoor mineral swimming pool. Milk River Bath is actually just over the parish border in Clarendon, about 30 miles (48km) southeast of Mandeville.
Open: daily 07.00–21.00hrs.

◆
SAVANNA-LA-MAR
Its name means 'plain by the sea', and this undistinguished market town and port – popularly known as Sav-la-Mar – is set on Westmoreland's south coast. The bustling wharf lies at the end of Great George Street, near the remaining walls of an old fort which now form an improvised swimming pool. Along this street you can see the 19th-century courthouse with its ornate drinking fountain and a variety of pavement stalls. It is a popular and pretty spot for bathing and picnicking. Savanna-la-Mar lies 75 miles (120km) west of Mandeville, and about 20 miles (32km) from Negril.

◆
MILK RIVER BATH
This mineral spa lies in a rural setting beside the Milk River. The therapeutic value of these waters was apparently discovered by a badly beaten slave who ran off to the hills, where he bathed his wounds in a salty spring; seeing the

◆◆◆
YS FALLS

Set in a beautiful green valley surrounded by rolling wooded hills, YS Falls are completely unspoilt – as nature intended – and, partly for that reason, are the most enchanting of Jamaica's waterfalls. After driving a short distance up a very rough lane from the main road (taking the turning at Holland, about 33 miles (53km) west of Mandeville), visitors should stop at a bar to buy a ticket and pick up a local guide. The falls are reached by walking across meadows, and through woods where there is only the sound of water splashing over rocks. Bathing is possible in the crystal-clear greenish pools. It is a stunning spot to picnic, swim or simply sit and soak up the scenery. The falls are best visited in the morning, as clouds tend to gather as the day goes on.

Natural grace at YS Falls

PEACE AND QUIET

Wildlife and Countryside in Jamaica
by Paul Sterry

A fiery Jamaican sunset

For those simply seeking relaxation and peace and quiet, Jamaica makes an ideal destination. However, for those who also have an interest in natural history, the island is a paradise. More than 250 species of bird have been recorded, of which 25 species and 21 sub-species are endemic; in other words they are found nowhere else in the world. In common with Jamaica's butterflies and flowers, many of the birds are extremely colourful, as one might imagine in so idyllic a place.

White sand beaches backed by groves of palm trees make the island a living picture of the ideal tropical island. In places around the coast there are also marshes and swamps, while, inland, there are steep mountains covered in luxuriant forest. Much of the original forest in the lowland areas has long since gone, cleared and replaced by the cultivation of crops such as mangos, bananas and sugar-cane.

The Coast

For most holiday visitors, the glorious, sandy beaches are Jamaica's crowning glory. However, the island's coastline is far from uniform: there are coastal lagoons, mudflats and mangroves, especially along the south coast, and rocky shores with offshore coral reefs along the northern coast. Each habitat attracts different types of wildlife, so there is always something to see wherever you are along the coast.

From the point of view of anyone interested in natural history, sandy beaches have least to offer, since they have few food resources and no shelter. However, above the tide-line, washed-up seashells can provide hours of interest

PEACE AND QUIET

Brown pelican

since there are so many different species to look for. Also, land crabs can be found on the coconut palms. Mudflats are rich in invertebrates, so when exposed at low tide, they provide much better feeding for birds and consequently better opportunities for the birdwatcher; look for egrets, herons, waders and terns. Further offshore, coral reefs are also extremely productive and many cays are located off Kingston, Negril and Portland on the south coast. Mangroves are an important habitat for many forms of wildlife. The salt-tolerant trees that make up the swamps tolerate immersion in seawater and exposure to air on a twice-daily basis with the tides. Their complex root-systems trap mud and help consolidate new land. Fiddler crabs and other crustaceans are abundant and

form the basis of the food web here. Mangroves are important nurseries for the young stages of many oceanic fish species.

Brown Pelican

Brown pelicans are common around the coasts, often displaying little fear of humans. They may look rather cumbersome on the ground, but in the air they are skilled and elegant fliers. This is the only species of pelican that dives to catch its food. If a shoal of fish is located, up to a dozen birds may gather in the vicinity, plunge-diving into the water, their throat pouches inflating to engulf the prey. Juvenile brown pelicans have mottled brown plumage. Adults, however, are more striking and have attractive markings on the head and neck. During the breeding season, the cap and lower neck are creamy buff while the nape of the neck is chestnut. Pelicans nest in mangroves from December until June.

The Blue Mountains

The Blue Mountains dominate eastern Jamaica. Much of the area is still cloaked in forest that is home to many of Jamaica's birds, although forestry and coffee plantations are regrettably depleting the natural vegetation. The main peaks lie along the Grand Ridge and include Blue Mountain Peak (7,402 feet; 2,255m) – the highest mountain in Jamaica.

The easiest point of access is from the Kingston Newcastle Buff Bay road; between Newcastle and Hardwar Gap, the forest is excellent. There are numerous trails leading from Newcastle itself and to the north of the town in the Hollywell National Recreation Park.

Continuing along the road to Buff Bay from Newcastle, turn off towards Westphalia and you will come in to the vicinity of the Cinchona Gardens; to reach these English-style gardens which are in the heart of a coffee-growing area requires a steep hike from the road.

Reaching the summit of Blue Mountain Peak requires considerable effort and a degree of planning. There are hostels near Mavis Bank (Whitfield Hall) and Pine Grove; information can be obtained from the Jamaica Tourist Board.

Luxuriant forests of blue mahoe – the national tree of Jamaica – and mahogany cover the mountains. Tree ferns and epiphytic orchids and bromeliads thrive in the

Humming-birds

Jamaica has four species of humming-birds, all of which are reasonably common and widespread. These delightful little birds are the only group that hover habitually, their wings looking like a blur of colour. Although they occasionally take insects, they feed for the most part on nectar, collecting it from flowers while on the wing; in the process they transfer pollen from one flower to another and are important agents of pollination for many of Jamaica's flowers. At only 2½ inches (6cm) in length, the vervain humming-bird is the smallest species on the island. The plumage is mainly green and the female has a white-tipped tail. There are two species of streamertail – black-billed and red-billed – males of which have long tail streamers. Lastly, the Jamaican mango is comparatively large at 5 inches (13cm) in length. The plumage is mainly dark, although a reddish sheen can be seen on the head in certain lights. Humming-birds build delicate little nests from lichens and cobwebs. Although in themselves the eggs are small, in relation to the size of the bird that produced them they are among the largest in the bird kingdom.

humidity and colourful butterflies abound.

Hellshire Hills

This region of arid limestone terrain cloaked in dense cactus scrub lies south of Spanish Town, within easy reach of Kingston. Popular sandy beaches can be found on the road to Fort Clarence and Hellshire Point, but the interior of the hills is largely inaccessible because of the inpenetrable scrub. Salt lagoons and mangrove swamps can be found along the road to Hellshire Point – look for herons, ibises and waders.

Marshall's Pen

Marshall's Pen is a private cattle ranch and nature reserve on the northwest outskirts of Mandeville. Visitors should contact Marshall's Pen, PO Box 58, Mandeville, Jamaica for arrangements; a small admission charge is made. Twenty-three of Jamaica's endemic birds have been seen in the limestone forest that surrounds the farm.

Cockpit Country

South of Falmouth, this is an area of extraordinary limestone scenery, known as *karst*, where, over millions of years, gentle erosion by mildly acidic rainwater has carved bizarre conical shapes and sinkholes. Much of the terrain is covered in wet forest and is, to all intents and purposes, inaccessible to all but the most experienced and determined. However, a rough road, suitable for four-wheel drive vehicles, crosses the eastern sector from Albert Town to Stewart Town. There are plenty of stopping places along this road; highlights to look out for include parrots, now rare because of the depredations of collectors.

Black River Morass

At the coastal town of Black River, in the southwest, the Broad River and Black River have created the Great Morass, the most extensive wetland on the island. The Upper Morass has been partly drained and altered, while the Lower Morass, nearest to the town, remains largely unaffected.

The coastline of the Lower Morass is fringed with mangroves which gradually give way inland, under increasingly freshwater conditions, to saltgrass marsh and finally wetland forest. This is the haunt of herons, ibises, West Indian whistling ducks and waders. American crocodiles, although scarce, are regularly seen on boat trips into the swamps from Black River, and manatees – rare and docile marine mammals that graze sea grasses – are sometimes seen at the mouth of the rivers. Despite drainage, many wetland birds can still be seen on Upper Morass, and the area can be viewed from the roads which surround it between Elim, Newton, East Lacovia and Wilton. Visitors should also drive southeast from Black River on the road to Pondside and on to Treasure Beach. There are ponds beside the road between Pondside and Williamsfield, and Great Pedro Pond near Treasure Beach is good for ducks, grebes and waders.

Rockland Sanctuary and Feeding Station

Birdwatchers will certainly want to visit the Rocklands

Bananaquits on a coffee plant

American Crocodile

American crocodiles are widespread in the warm seas of the Caribbean although they have become rather scarce because of persecution. They can grow to an immense size – often over 12 feet (4m) in length – and prefer to live in coastal waters and estuaries.
Crocodiles spend much of their time in water with only the nose and eyes exposed to the air, although they do occasionally sunbathe. Females lay a clutch of eggs in soft sand beside the water and these are incubated by the warmth of the sun. American crocodiles can be distinguished from alligators because the fourth tooth on the lower jaw can still be seen when the mouth is closed.

Feeding Station, which can be reached along a track east from Anchovy, itself south of Montego Bay. This private sanctuary is owned by Miss Lisa Salmon; visitors are welcome between 15.00hrs and 17.00hrs, and there is a small entrance fee. The birds come to be fed and many are incredibly tame.

Three species of humming-bird can be seen here: red-billed streamertails, vervain humming-birds and Jamaican mangos. Visitors should also look for white-eyed thrushes and white-chinned thrushes. The former have prominent white eyes, brown heads bordered with a white half-collar, dark upperparts and pale underparts. White-chinned thrushes, on the other hand, have mainly dark plumage with a white spot on the wings and under the 'chin' and an attractive orange bill and legs.

Ocho Rios

Despite its popularity, there are plenty of opportunities to observe wildlife around Ocho Rios. The Shaw Park Botanical Gardens can be reached by heading south on the A3 and after a short distance turning right at the Anglican Church. Here visitors will find waterfalls, beautiful gardens, humming-birds and many other birds. The gardens of Carinosa are also worth visiting and have a walk-in aviary. By heading south on the A3, the visitor soon drives through Fern Gully, one of the best places on the island to see a wide variety of species of these attractive plants. To the west of Ocho Rios is the Dunn's River Falls, the best known and most spectacular waterfall on the island.

Eastern Jamaica

The eastern coast is one of the most dramatic and scenic parts of the island, and the coast road, which runs from Port Antonio to Morant Bay, allows easy exploration of the area. Heading southeast from Port Antonio, visitors soon reach the Blue Hole, an impressive but extremely popular tourist spot. As you continue around the coast, look for seabirds offshore, including white-tailed tropic birds between Machioneal and Hector's River. These graceful birds have white plumage and boast extremely long tail streamers. Sea birds can also be seen from near Morant Point Lighthouse, the most southeasterly point on Jamaica.

Frigatebirds

Magnificent frigatebirds are a familiar sight in the skies around the coast of Jamaica. These masters of the air have a wingspan over seven feet (2m) and effortlessly ride the sea breezes, using their long, forked tails to help control their direction. Sometimes called 'Man O' War' birds, frigatebirds are aerial pirates: although they sometimes scavenge dead fish and occasionally pick live ones from the surface of the water, most of their diet is obtained by harassing pelicans and other sea birds into disgorging their last meal. For their size, frigatebirds are lightweight; this helps minimise the effort required to remain airborne. Male frigatebirds have all-black plumage but have a throat sac which is bright red. When displaying to attract a female, this is inflated and is an extraordinary sight, especially when several males are nesting in the same area.

Shaw Park Botanical Gardens

FOOD AND DRINK

Visitors attracted by the beaches and the climate may not have realised that Jamaican cuisine can make eating one of the greatest pleasures of their holiday. Like so many aspects of life on the island, it derives much from the rich blend of cultural influences – from African to Arawak Indian, Spanish to Chinese, East Indian to English – as well as having a uniquely piquant Jamaican flavour. The island is blessed with a wide variety of fruit and vegetables, and its waters yield a wealth of fish and seafood.

You can eat well in the smallest roadside restaurant – bars and snack shacks – where standards of cleanliness and hygiene are high, so do not be put off even if they look shabby. You can often eat better (and much more cheaply) at many of the simple Jamaican guest houses than in sophisticated hotels – both of which serve meals to non-residents, except the all-inclusive hotels.

In a small local restaurant there is usually a blackboard with the day's menu displayed – which depends on what they managed to buy in the market or from the fishermen that morning. Food is often cooked to order and served at Jamaican pace, but usually worth the wait. As everywhere, there are also fast-food places to suit American and European impatience. Beside the road, you will notice the rondavel bars (a round or polygonal building with a pointed roof and sides that are open to breezes), which serve good snacks like jerk pork or chicken. In this climate, many restaurants have open-air terraces and patios. There is a variety of specialist restaurants too, such as Chinese or Rastafarian.

Ackee and salt fish is Jamaica's national dish – typically served for breakfast, but also as a snack at any time. Ackee is a bright red fruit that is seen growing on trees all over the island; it has to be allowed to ripen and open up naturally – to reveal three large black seeds set in lobes of yellow flesh, which is then boiled, otherwise it is poisonous. Cooked with salted cod and often mixed with onions and peppers, it's delicious – remarkably like scrambled eggs.

For breakfast and other meals you may also see 'run down' (run dun), which is mackerel, shad or salted cod simmered in boiled-down coconut milk, often with onions and peppers. Liver is another sustaining dish served for Jamaica-style breakfasts, as are fried slices of plantain. Hotels offer traditional, European or American dishes at breakfast, but the menu may also include fresh tropical fruit, and sweet things like cinnamon cakes or banana bread. Brown bread (or brown sugar) are almost never seen in Jamaica, though they have a type of bread called hard-dough (hardo) with a very close, hard texture. Soup is very popular in local

FOOD AND DRINK

Bright bites at a jerk pork bar

restaurants and is often automatically served before the main course, without being ordered. Staple spicy soups include pumpkin, red pea (bean) and pepperpot soup. Manish water is a highly-seasoned thick soup based on green bananas and goat offal. The seafood is superb. There is a wonderful variety of fresh fish, such as kingfish (usually served in steaks), various snapper (including red and yellow fin) and jack (rather like fresh pilchard). They are cooked in a variety of ways; small local restaurants, including shacks by the roadside or beaches, cook traditionally on open-fire stoves. Fried fish is generally not at all greasy but more like grilled fish, and it is often cooked in reduced coconut oil. Fried fish is often eaten with bammy – fried cassava bread. Peppered shrimp are a delicious delicacy of the Black River area. Lobster is universally popular.

Curried dishes, especially goat curry, are popular, and full of flavour (a way of cooking that Indian workers introduced). More conservative meat-eaters will easily find beef on menus. Roast suckling pig is another local speciality well worth trying, as is the jerk pork. Hot and spicy, it is traditionally cooked over a fire of pimento wood, which lies in a hollow or 'pit' – the most authentic and best is said to come from around Boston Bay, although it is sold everywhere. 'Jerk', by the way, comes from a Spanish word meaning to prepare the pork like the Quechua Indians of South America. Jerk pork and other savoury snacks are often eaten with fried dumplings, called festival or johnny cakes.

In local restaurants main courses are typically served with rice 'n' peas (white rice with red kidney beans, or occasionally green gunga peas, cooked in coconut milk) – such a staple food that it has been dubbed 'the Jamaican coat-of-arms'. Sweet potato is particularly good with curries;

green banana, breadfruit and yam are bland, starchy vegetables which are fine to accompany spicy foods. Green vegetables which may be new to you include callaloo, okra, and chocho (pear-shaped with a pale green, prickly skin and a taste like marrow).

For dessert, try the romantically-named matrimony: a delectable blend of orange and star apple pulp mixed with cream, sugar and nutmeg. Guava cheese is a sweet chewy jelly.

The wealth of fruit available is a mouthwatering delight: pineapple, pawpaw (papaya), bananas, mango, guava, watermelon, passion fruit and many others not found in supermarkets at home – succulent fruits sounding and tasting exotic. Ortaniques are a cross between an orange and a tangerine – Jamaica has successfully produced many hybrid citrus fruits.

Snacks which may be unfamiliar include Solomon Grundy, a spiced pickled herring often served as an appetizer, as is tasty smoked marlin. Stamp-and-go are crispy batter-fried salt codfish fritters; the name comes from an old nautical command that used to be given to sailors. If you visit a Jamaican home you may be offered a slice of rich, dark, fruity Christmas cake – so heavily laced with rum it improves with age. Locals often chew on a length of sugar cane – usually larger and softer than the cane used to make sugar and rum – bought from wayside stalls. After having the cane stripped, you suck or chew the stringy interior.

Drinks

Starting with the strong stuff: Jamaica equals rum. There is a wide range of different colours, tastes and strengths – Appleton is the most famous brand. Gold rum has a light, smooth flavour which is good for drinking on the rocks. The longer the rum has been matured in oak barrels, the mellower (and more expensive) it becomes. Many Jamaicans drink the potent white overproof rum – tradition

A hearty Jamaican breakfast

FOOD AND DRINK

has it that the first gulp opens the eyes, the second closes them. Rum is also used in many delicious cocktails, like Planters' Punch. These are frequently very sweet, so if you prefer them less so ask the barman to hold back (or leave out) the syrup. Jamaican liqueurs include coffee-flavoured Tia Maria, a rum liqueur called Rumona, and Sangster's Old Jamaica liqueurs which are blended with rum and come in several varieties such as Blue Mountain coffee, ginger and ortanique. The most popular local beer is Red Stripe. Imported wines tend to be expensive, but there are wines made in Jamaica from imported pulp – Monterey and the slightly drier Rhine Valley are white wines reminiscent of popular German wines. With such a profusion of fresh fruit, there is also an exciting choice of non-alcoholic fruit cocktails. A traditional soft drink is sorrel, which is flavoured with ginger – it tastes like ginger-blackcurrant squash. Soursop is also an old favourite, made from a rough-skinned fruit of that name. Irish Moss is a healthy blend of processed seaweed (agar), condensed milk, vanilla and nutmeg – an alleged aid to sexual prowess. Water is generally served with meals, and is quite safe to drink from the tap. Remember that in a hot climate it is advisable to drink plenty of liquid – without alcohol.

Jamaica's Blue Mountain coffee is renowned for its strong, aromatic flavour; make sure you ask for it, as many places simply serve instant.

Crafts with character – the Royal Dwarf Factory

SHOPPING

Jamaican handicrafts are widely sold in the north coast resorts – and at stalls along the roadside. All the main resorts and towns visited by tourists have their craft market, selling goods such as wooden carvings, woven straw hats and baskets, tie-dyed clothes, shell jewellery, or beads and belts in Rasta colours. Do not buy jewellery made from black coral or from turtles since both of these are protected. In these markets you should haggle to buy at a good price, but do not be hassled into buying souvenirs you don't want; the 'higglers' are expert at high-pressure selling both in these markets and on the street. If you are self-catering, it is well worth visiting the ordinary fruit and vegetable markets. But even if you are not buying, these bustling street markets make for a colourful taste of real Jamaica – and there is less hassle, as the food markets cater for locals rather than tourists. Market women are still called 'higglers', though this also refers to any street hawkers. Details on craft markets are given under individual resorts, along with shops where you can find some higher quality Jamaican artwork. Two very picturesque places to find some attractive gifts, including arts and crafts, are Devon House in Kingston and Harmony Hall near Ocho Rios.

The vogue in Jamaica, as in so many places, is for modern shopping plazas. Some of these are aimed specifically at tourists, with shops selling duty-free goods and up-market boutiques; other centres have more everyday items. Banks, pharmacies and supermarkets can often be found in or around one of the shopping plazas. The duty-free shops are widely advertised. (Information on places to shop is given under individual resorts; for shop opening hours, see page 123 in the **Directory**.)

Popular souvenirs worth taking home from Jamaica include rum (naturally), local liqueurs such as Tia Maria or Sangster's Old Jamaica, Blue Mountain coffee, and reggae tapes or records.

ACCOMMODATION

All the resorts have an excellent range of accommodation. However, the choice is much more limited in the southern half of the island. The Tourist Board has a list of 'approved' accommodation, including guest houses (although some of the small, more out-of-the-way places may not have been bothered to register with the Tourist Board, as they fear paying extra tax, so it does not necessarily mean that the Tourist Board has found standards unacceptable if a place is not on their list). The variety of accommodation is not widely publicised; tour operators tend to use certain standard hotels, and often exclude the cheaper ones.

ACCOMMODATION

Greengrocer, Montego Bay

Generally accommodation *is* expensive if, for example, you are used to Mediterranean prices. It is possible to find relatively low-priced hotels, guest houses or lodgings, but you will probably have to book independently. If you are willing to take pot luck, you can often just ask around on the spot in smaller towns and villages (for example, in local shops) and find a simple, basic room for the night – even in a private home, where the family wants to make extra cash. You *can* make your stay in Jamaica reasonably inexpensive if you are prepared to be flexible and a bit adventurous. Prices are lower in summer – except in Kingston. A room tax is charged, which varies depending on the season and category of hotel, and a 10 per cent service charge is usually added on top of this.

The popular tourist hotels tend to have an American approach (for instance, half-board is called MAP – modified American plan), and prices are quoted in US dollars. There has been a boom in all-inclusive hotels, where everything – including sports, tips and even drinks and cigarettes in most places – is 'free' after paying the initial all-in price. This may sound like a good deal, but it discourages guests from setting foot outside the hotel. If all you are interested in is the beach, with hot and cold running sports and activities all day long, this may be ideal. Many of the larger hotels are attractively designed around lovely tropical gardens, often behind a private beach. Most hotels have air-conditioning, or ceiling fans in cheaper places (except the most basic). Even very simple accommodation is usually very clean, and service is typically willing and friendly. Check with the Tourist Board about which of the larger hotels have a booking agent representing them in your country.

Jamaica also offers self-catering accommodation, from modest rooms with a kitchenette or hot-plate and fridge, to sumptuous villas with a maid to cook and clean as well as a gardener. For information on these contact the Tourist Board or the Jamaica Association of Villas and Apartments (JAVA) at Pineapple Place, Box 298, Ocho Rios, St Ann (tel: 974-2508).

For information on campsites, cabins and budget lodgings on the island contact Peter Bentley, Maya, Box 216, Kingston 7, Jamaica (tel: 927 2097). The Jamaica Tourist Board offices will also be able to help you with enquiries.

NIGHTLIFE AND ENTERTAINMENT

Much of the island's nightlife is based around the main tourist resorts and hotels – and in these spots, you'll be able to give your dancing shoes a good workout. Larger hotels, especially the all-inclusives, have nightly entertainment – anything from a calypso singer to a live band, fashion show or the full works with limbo-dancing and fire-eating. Some of the discos, nightclubs and other evening entertainments are listed under individual resorts. Being the cultural centre of Jamaica, Kingston has a wide choice of entertainment. Outside the main resorts and towns, there may not be much to do at night apart from hang out at the local bar – which can turn out to be quite an entertainment in itself.

Poolside drinks at the Wyndham Rose Hall hotel (see page 22)

WEATHER AND WHEN TO GO

Winter and summer seasons are a bit of a misnomer in Jamaica as temperatures throughout the year only vary within a range of around 80°F (27°C) to 90°F (32°C). The coolest months are December to March; the driest February and March; the wettest in spring (May to June) and autumn (September to October), but only to the extent of daily tropical showers. There is quite a variance in local climate on the island caused by the high peaks of the central Blue Mountain range, which divides the relatively humid and rainy north coast from the drier southern districts. The highest annual rainfall is found in the east of the island. Humidity is generally high, but mercifully tempered by a cool tradewind off the ocean, known as the Doctor's Wind, during the day,

and an evening breeze from the mountains, the ominously named Undertaker's Wind, in the evening. If the heat and humidity gets too much, a trip to the interior should bring relief with temperatures 10°F to 20°F lower than those on the coast. A local rhyme has this to say about hurricanes: 'June, too soon. July, stand by. August, prepare you must. September, remember. October, all over'. Hurricanes in June, July or October tend to last for around a week; in August and September they can run for a fortnight. If the situation is serious, the Office of Disaster Preparedness and Emergency Relief Coordination (ODIPERC) will broadcast warnings and instructions on television and radio. High season in Jamaica is mid-December to Easter, particularly around Christmas and the New Year when hotel rooms, rental cars and beach space are at a premium.

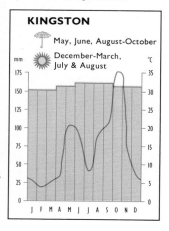

KINGSTON

☂ May, June, August-October

☀ December-March, July & August

HOW TO BE A LOCAL

Jamaicans are generally good natured and exuberant – they like to laugh a lot. You can have great fun returning their friendliness and chatting to them – they love to talk, too. However, in tourist resorts persistent hassling can be annoying; tourists equals money, and you have to remember that this is a poor country, and everyone is anxious to earn a crust. If you are being hassled to buy goods or services you don't want, just keep saying a polite but firm 'no, thank you'. Jamaicans appreciate directness; they are very direct themselves so do not find the blunt truth offensive. Misunderstandings are more likely to arise if you couch what you mean in evasiveness and equivocation. This does not mean you can be downright rude: as everywhere, good manners and a smile go a long way in oiling the wheels of social encounters. 'Do as you would be done by' is a motto tourists will find it advisable to adopt. In rural areas, Jamaicans are usually simply curious about white visitors. Contact with the locals on an equal basis can be a most rewarding experience. If you'd like an introduction, ask the Tourist Board about their (free) Meet The People scheme; and Diana McIntyre-Pike of the Astra Hotel in Mandeville is also eager to put visitors in touch with locals. Although some of the larger resorts and towns seem to be full of bustling activity, Jamaicans have an unruffled, relaxed attitude. 'No problem – this is Jamaica', they'll say. It overcomes the breakdowns and delays that inevitably occur in services such as trains, buses, telephones, and so on – which in Western eyes seem to stem from lack of organisation. Even if there does seem to be a problem, they'll shrug and tell you 'no problem'. Since impatient demands for service and loud protestations will yield few results, your visit will be much more relaxing if you settle into the Jamaican pace of life – content in the knowledge that eventually most things 'soon come'.

Jamaicans may be relaxed, but there is one aspect of behaviour where anything does *not* go – or rather nothing, because that's nude sunbathing. Going topless has become acceptable, and is frequently seen on tourist beaches, although local women do not do it. Sunbathing in the nude will cause offence, except on certain private beaches that are reserved for the purpose.

Women travelling on their own are more than likely to be approached by men who can become a pest. The Jamaicans are as direct about sex as everything else; if that's what they are after, they will ask you almost straight away if you want to 'spend the night' with them. Don't be coy, your response must be just as direct in order to prevent misunderstandings. If the answer is 'no', don't try to let them down gently, as that is more likely to lead to trouble than saying so straight out. The chances are you will be offered *ganja* (marijuana) or even cocaine. Just remember that these drugs are illegal, and if you are caught with any in your possession it could result in a hefty fine, deportation or even a jail sentence.

CHILDREN

Jamaicans love children – in fact, Jamaican women advise having lots, with or without a husband. Children are a good point of contact when striking up conversations with locals. However, some of the smarter hotels do not accept children as guests – including some of the all-inclusive hotels which are for couples only, like the Sandals group. On the other hand, there are also all-inclusive hotels which are specifically aimed at families – with special packages and activities – such as Boscobel Beach not far from Ocho Rios, the Trelawny Beach Hotel at Falmouth (east of Montego

Bay), or the Franklyn D Resort at Runaway Bay. Generally, children are more welcome at the smaller, less expensive hotels and guest houses – and in some of these, children under a certain age (12, for example) can stay in their parents' room free. Of the main resorts, Negril would be a good one for children: it has a superb beach and safe swimming.

Children might find some of the typical local dishes in Jamaica a bit spicy, but you can easily find food they will like – including fried chicken, burgers and fruity puddings. Few of the sights are likely to interest children very much. But plenty of fun can be had outdoors with lots of watersports, swimming and sandcastles. You must watch out for sunburn, which can ruin a holiday. The sun in Jamaica is strong, and cooling breezes deceptive, particularly for tender young skin. Make sure you have long-sleeved T-shirts, sunhats and sunblock cream to hand. And make sure your children don't stay out too long, especially in the first few days – the same goes for you.

TIGHT BUDGET TIPS

● Hotel prices out of season (May to December) are likely to be as much as 40% cheaper.

● The south is generally cheaper than the north.

● The big resorts are the most expensive, so stay and shop in the smaller places.

● Restaurants are cheaper than hotels.

● Shop around for car rental.

● Bring your own toiletries, film, etc – as they are likely to cost more if you buy them in Jamaica.

● Rates of exchange are cheaper in banks than hotels or *bureaux de change*.

SPORT

There are plenty of sporting activities to be found in the main resorts and at larger hotels – again, especially at the all-inclusives. Watersports of every description reign supreme at Negril, Montego Bay and Ocho Rios, with a good variety also at Runaway Bay, Port Antonio and Kingston. You can go sailing, waterskiing, windsurfing, scuba diving, snorkelling, jetskiing, parasailing, deep-sea fishing, you name it – and instruction is often available. If you have snorkelling equipment, it's a good idea to take it with you. Further details of specific sporting activities are given under individual resorts.

DIRECTORY

Contents

Arriving

Entry formalities British visitors require a valid 10-year passport and return ticket, but no visa, for stays of up to six months; EEC residents can stay for up to three months without a visa; North American citizens can remain for up to six months, and can replace the passport requirement with two documents from the following list: residency card or naturalisation certificate, driver's licence with photograph, voter's registration card or birth certificate. Married women will require their marriage

Getting about in style: jet skiing in Montego Bay

certificate if producing a birth certificate from the above list.

Airports

Jamaica has two international airports. Kingston's Norman Manley International airport serves the island's capital and the resorts of Mandeville and Port Antonio, while Montego Bay has its own Donald Sangster International Airport, which is also more convenient for visitors to Negril and Ocho Rios.

Transport from the Airport

Taxis are readily available and suggested tariffs to various

DIRECTORY

destinations are displayed in the airport building. Fares should be agreed before you set forth. If possible, it is best to arrange airport transportation to your hotel with a travel agent in advance. Although fares from the airports into Kingston or Montego Bay are reasonable, it will be far more costly to reach the outlying resorts.

Babysitting

Most hotels will be able to provide a 'nursemaid' service.

Bicycle Rental

Car rental (see below) is an expensive business in Jamaica, and outside the main centres public transport is pretty dire. If you are not planning on a major sightseeing expedition, a motorbike or moped could be the answer for local journeys. Most hotels can arrange bike rental, or try:

Western Bike Rental, Montego Bay (tel: 952-0185)
Stony Hill Castle Ltd Bike Rentals, Negril (tel: 957-4460)
Motor Trails, Ocho Rios (tel: 974-5058)

Camping

There are several campsites in the Blue Mountains, and also around the main resorts. For information on sites, maps, treks and other budget accommodation contact:
Jamaica Alternative and Camping-Hiking Association (JACHA), Box 216, Kingston 7 (tel: 927-2097).

Car Rental

Car rental is expensive in Jamaica, and during the winter season it is sometimes difficult to get a rental car at short notice. It is advisable to book ahead at any time, and plan your sightseeing itinerary carefully to get best value for money. A major credit card imprint will suffice for a deposit; without one you may have to lodge upwards of J$ 3,000 in cash. Foreign driving licences are valid for up to three months; and there is a minimum age limit of 21 years. Most major car rental companies are represented on the island, so you can book before you leave home. They, and local companies, are listed in Jamaica's Yellow Pages telephone directory, and most have offices in Kingston, Montego Bay and the main resorts. Some useful numbers are:
Budget (tel: 952-2091)
Caribbean Car Rentals (tel: 926-6339)
Island Car Rentals (tel: 926-8012)
National (tel: 952-2650)
Trifty Rent-A-Car (tel: 952-4585)

Chemists see Pharmacies

Crime

Petty theft is a way of life in Jamaica, and the locals suffer too. Thefts are rarely violent, but unguarded possessions will disappear in the twinkle of an eye. Common sense dictates that you leave any valuables locked in the hotel safe, wear your camera around your neck, and use a money belt instead of a fat wallet in a back pocket. Report losses to the police immediately. Though there is little chance of your property being recovered, a police report will assist with insurance claims.

Customs Regulations

Duty free allowances on arrival in Jamaica are: 200 cigarettes or 50 cigars or ½lb of tobacco; 1 litre of wine; and one litre of spirits. Restricted items include plants, flowers, meat, fruit and vegetables. Jamaican currency (the Jamaican dollar) cannot be imported or exported from the island. Foreign currency and travellers' cheques must be exchanged for local currency at airports, banks and hotels. (For further details, see **Money Matters**.)

Departure Tax

There is a J$100 departure tax payable at the airport when you leave.

Disabled People

The Jamaica Tourist Board has details of hotels with facilities for disabled visitors. These all feature ramps, adapted bathrooms and reserved parking spaces. Make careful enquiries before you book your hotel, as many have steep cliff paths down to the beach. Hotels in Negril usually have better access as they tend to be built on a single level.

Drugs

Marijuana (*ganja*) is a major Jamaican export crop, but it is also illegal. Dealers will approach you in the street or on the beach, and the drug is easily accessible. However, penalties are stiff, with a first-offence conviction for possession leading to a hefty fine and possible imprisonment or deportation.

Driving

Jamaicans drive on the left. Simple speed restrictions are enforced with a 30mph (48kph) limit in town, and a 50mph (80kph) limit on the highway. Outside city centres, the roads are fairly basic with tortuous twists and turns, few signs and bone-shaking potholes. Leave plenty of extra time for car journeys – you will get nowhere in a hurry. Car horns are a popular form of greeting, as well as warning, so do not take offence. People standing by the roadside waving their arms are not threatening, but asking for a lift. Fuel stations are generally open Monday to Saturday 07.30 to 19.00hrs; most are closed on Sunday and sometimes Wednesday. Do not expect to use a credit card.

Electricity

110-220 volts, 50 cycles AC.

Embassies and Consulates

Australia: Australian High Commission, Kingston (tel: 926 3550)
Canada: Canadian High Commission, 30 Knutsford Boulevard, Kingston 5 (tel: 926 1500)
UK: British High Commission, 26 Trafalgar Road, Kingston 5 (tel: 926 9050)
US: United States Embassy, 2 Oxford Road, Kingston 5 (tel: 929 4850)

Emergency Telephone Numbers

Ambulance and Fire
    Department: 110
Police and Air-Sea Rescue: 119

Entertainment Information

Events are well advertised in Jamaica. Jamaica Tourist Board offices in all the main centres can provide information over the counter, as can your hotel; or consult the entertainments section of *The Daily Gleaner*, which also publishes a monthly guide.

Health

There are no vaccination requirements for Jamaica, but it is advisable to check with a tropical disease unit, your airline or travel agent in case any precautions have been recommended. They may advise Polio, Tetanus, Typhoid and Hepatitis vaccinations. Tap water is drinkable and standards of hygiene are generally good. Mosquitoes can be a real problem, so do not stint on the insect repellant. Birth-control is not a big issue in Jamaica, and the use of condoms limited, which has led to an alarming incidence of heterosexual AIDS. Government hospitals in Kingston and Mandeville provide medical services at reasonable rates, but it is always recommended to take out full health insurance before you leave home. Jamaican sun is potent stuff, so bring an adequate supply of sunblock.

Holidays (Public and Religious)

New Year's Day: 1 January
Ash Wednesday
Good Friday
Easter Monday
Labor Day: 23 May
Independence Day: first
  Monday in August
National Hero's Day: third
  Monday in October
Christmas Day: 25 December
Boxing Day: 26 December

Clarendon Plains

prices are often quoted in US dollars, and US currency is accepted legally in hotels and illegally in numerous stores. Purchases in duty-free shops must be paid for in foreign currency. Major credit cards and travellers' cheques are widely accepted in tourist-orientated retail outlets, good restaurants and hotels, but check first and do not expect fuel stations or smaller eating places to be prepared. When exchanging currency ask for small denomination bills – it is often difficult to get change.

Media
The best local paper is *The Daily Gleaner. The Jamaica Record* is also a daily, and *The Star* an evening tabloid. There is one television station, which dishes out a menu of US soaps; plus a handful of local radio stations with a greater preponderance of phone-in chat shows than reggae.

Money Matters
The Jamaican dollar cannot be imported or exported to or from the island. You must cash foreign currency or travellers' cheques at banks, *bureaux de change* or your hotel, and then keep the receipt in order to reconvert currency before you leave. Banks offer the best rates. The Jamaican dollar divides into 100 cents. There are 1, 5, 10, 20, 25, 50 and J$1 coins, and 1, 2, 5, 10, 20, 50 and 100 dollar bills. In tourist areas

Opening Times
Banks
Monday to Thursday 09.00 to 14.00hrs, Friday 09.00 to 12.00 and 14.30 to 17.00hrs.
Businesses
Normal business hours are Monday to Friday 08.30 or 09.00 to 16.30 or 17.00hrs. Offices are closed on weekends.
Shopping
Generally Monday to Friday 08.30 or 09.00 to 17.00hrs, Saturday until 18.00hrs. In tourist areas there is usually plenty of opportunity for shopping on Sunday; half-days are sometimes observed on Wednesday (Kingston), Thursday (Montego Bay), or Friday (Ocho Rios).

Personal Safety
This is largely a matter of common sense in Jamaica. (See **Crime**.) It is unwise to carry large amounts of cash or valuables, and foolish to enter the shantytown areas of West

Kingston, such as Trench Town. Women travelling alone are likely to receive several good-natured propositions: a polite 'no thanks' will probably suffice.

Pharmacies

Pharmacies are plentiful in Jamaica, and most sell a wide range of goods, such as sweets and newspapers, beachballs and gifts, in addition to medicines and toiletries.

Places of Worship

According to the *Guiness Book of Records*, Jamaica boasts more churches per square mile than any other country in the world. Anglicans, Adventists, Baptists, Methodists and Roman Catholics will find churches throughout the island; Jamaica's only synagogue is in Kingston.

Police

The Jamaican police force is supposedly up to its collective neck in the island's drug problem, and there is little chance of recovering stolen goods. Otherwise, police are helpful with directions, and sympathetic when filling out theft reports. In an emergency tel: 119.

Postal Services

Jamaica is well supplied with post offices, but deliveries are slow and can take up to a week within the island itself. Overseas mail is likely to be equally slow. Post offices are open during normal business hours; there are no home deliveries, so all mail is addressed to and collected from post office box numbers.

Public Transport

Air

Trans Jamaica Airlines operate an internal flight service linking Kingston, Montego Bay, Negril, Ocho Rios and Port Antonio. Prices are reasonable and tickets can be booked direct or through a travel agent.

Bus and Minibus

Single-deck 'Coaster' buses (more comfortable) and minibuses are a cheap method of transport around the island, but services are unreliable and departures erratic at best. Drivers will not leave the bus station unless the vehicle is full, and by that they mean packed out. The Jamaica Tourist Board offices have schedules and fare information.

Taxis

Taxis are easily located at airports and hotels, or can be hailed in the street. They display red PPV (Public Passenger Vehicle) plates; some have an additional 'Tourism' plate which indicates that they have passed a more rigorous inspection. Rates are regulated, but if a taxi is not metered agree on a price before you set off. Hotels usually have a list of set fares, and suggested rates are displayed at airports. A 25 per cent surcharge is payable on rides between 24.00 and 05.00hrs; drivers also expect a tip.

Trains

There are two services a day between Kingston and Montego Bay. The inexpensive five-hour journey makes a pleasant change, and there is first class (also very cheap) travel on Sunday.

Telephones

There are public telephones in most areas (Treasure Beach excepted), but it is easier to make an international call than raise a number in the next town. Public telephones take 10 cent coins and phone cards. If you are using coins, have at least two 10 cent coins ready to insert when the other party answers the telephone. (You do not insert money before you dial.) Phone cards are available from telephone company offices and other authorised outlets, such as pharmacies and fuel stations. If you are making an overseas call it is best to have a phone card, or call collect. All overseas calls must go through the operator; any calls made from hotels will attract a hefty surcharge. To call Jamaica from the UK dial 0101 809, followed by the subscriber's number.

Useful telephone numbers:

Directory assistance: dial 114
Local inter-island call operator: dial 112
International call operator: dial 113

Time

Jamaica is GMT minus six hours in spring/summer; and GMT minus five hours in autumn/winter. Jamaican time is the same as US Eastern Standard time all year.

Tipping

Tipping is widely expected in Jamaica. Most hotels add a 10-12½ per cent service charge for meals and bar bills; restaurants will add around 10-15 per cent; but staff still expect a small gratuity.

Buses: cheap but unpredictable

Although you pay upfront for a guided tour or raft trip, you should also tip your guide. Jamaicans expect photographers to ask permission before taking snaps of them, and a small tip.

Tourist Information

For information before you leave home, contact the Jamaica Tourist Board's overseas offices in:
Canada: 1 Eglinton Avenue East, Suite 616, Toronto M4P 3A1 tel: (416) 482-7850
UK and Europe: 111 Gloucester Place, London W1H 3PH tel: (071) 224-0505
US: 866 Second Avenue, 10th Floor, New York, NY 10017 tel: (212) 688-7650
The Tourist Board has local offices at:
21 Dominica Drive, Kingston 5 tel: 929-9200
21 Ward Avenue, Mandeville tel: 962-1072
Cornwall Beach, Montego Bay tel: 952-4425
Shop 9, Adrija Plaza, Negril tel: 957-4243
Ocean Village Shopping Centre, Ocho Rios tel: 974-2570
City Centre Plaza, Port Antonio tel: 993-3051

LANGUAGE

Jamaica is, of course, an English-speaking country. So you may be surprised to find that the language you commonly hear spoken is virtually incomprehensible. The colourful Jamaican patois has evolved from a wealth of different cultural influences over the centuries – its roots lie in 17th-century English, with a blend of regional British intonations (like Welsh and Scottish) and West African words, expressions, grammatical structure and pronunciation. More recently the Rastafarian dialect has crept into common speech; some of their words have 'I' substituted at the beginning, due to their emphasis on the importance of the individual. The following examples will give you a little taste of Jamaican patois – it includes some unfamiliar words plus a few phonetic spellings of (more-or-less) English words and phrases:

Babylon the established order (Church, State, the West), or figures of authority like the police

bangarang baggage

ben dung plaza stalls set out on the pavement (bend down plaza)

big gill a little more than ¼ pint (75ml)

bo-bo foolish person

boonoonoonoos delightful, the best

bredrin Rasta brothers

a chain not far (literally 22 yards)

cho man (mon) never mind, no problem

clot cloth

dat that

de gal dem the girls

de house dem the houses

dreadlocks Rasta locks of hair

duppy ghost

herb ('erb) ganja, marijuana

I an' I we

irie in harmony with the universe, just right, great

isire desire

ital natural, pure foods or lifestyle

ivine divine

labrish discussion

likkle little

maga (maaga) thin woman

mash up (op) badly beaten, break, in turmoil

me wan fi go don ton I want to go downtown

mumpy fat woman

nyam to eat

one love Rasta greeting or parting expression

putta-putta mud

rass backside (either very rude or affectionate)

riddim rhythm

soon come sometime sooner or later, take your time

teet teeth

tenky thank you

walk good parting expression

wha fi do what to do

yea man (mon) yes (very commonly used for agreement, to men and women)

INDEX

INDEX/ACKNOWLEDGEMENTS

The Automobile Association wishes to thank the following photographers and libraries for their assistance in the preparation of this book.

ROY VICTOR took all the photographs (©AA PHOTO LIBRARY) except:

INTERNATIONAL PHOTOBANK Cover Ocho Rios, 53 Prospect Plantation.

JAMES DAVIS TRAVEL PHOTOGRAPHY 34 Greenwood Great House, 66 Somerset Falls.

MARY EVANS PICTURE LIBRARY 14 Rebellion.

NATURE PHOTOGRAPHERS LTD 104 Pelican (P R Sterry), 107 Bananaquits (W S Paton).

SPECTRUM COLOUR LIBRARY 59 Port Antonio Harbour, 80 Limbo dancer, 83 Blue Mountain Peak.

A. WILSON 88 Spanish Town, 96 Treasure Beach.